SOMERSET MYSTERIES

Polly Lloyd and Michael Williams

BOSSINEY BOOKS

ACKNOWLEDGEMENTS

Front cover photography: ROY WESTLAKE
Front cover design: MAGGIE GINGER
Back cover photography: JULIA DAVEY
Other photographs: RAY BISHOP, JULIA DAVEY, POLLY LLOYD,
ROY WESTLAKE, FELICITY YOUNG
Drawings: FELICITY YOUNG

First published in 1991
by Bossiney Books, St Teath, Bodmin, Cornwall.

Typeset and printed by Penwell Print, Callington, Cornwall.

© Michael Williams and Polly Lloyd

ISBN 0 948158 71 9

Introducing Michael Williams – and the book

*M*ICHAEL WILLIAMS, *a Cornishman, started full-time publishing in 1975. He and his wife Sonia live in a cottage on the shoulder of a green valley just outside St Teath in North Cornwall.*

In addition to publishing and writing, Michael Williams is a keen cricketer and collector of cricket books and autographs. He was the first captain of the Cornish Crusaders Cricket Club and is today President of the Crusaders. He is also a member of Cornwall and Gloucestershire County Cricket Clubs. A member of the R.S.P.C.A. and the International League for the Protection of Horses, he has worked hard for reform in laws relating to animal welfare. In 1984 he was elected to The Ghost Club, and is convinced Cornwall is the most haunted area in the whole of Great Britain.

His latest title is Supernatural Search in Cornwall, *and his earlier publications include* Paranormal in the Westcountry *and* Superstition & Folklore. *As a publisher, he now operates in six areas: Cornwall, Devon, Somerset, Avon, Dorset and Wiltshire.*

In this, Bossiney's 201st title, Michael Williams and Polly Lloyd, the well-known broadcaster and television personality, explore Somerset Mysteries. *They visit haunted properties and discuss the significance of ley lines. They take a look at the shaping of Somerset and the Glastonbury Zodiac. Why is Somerset such a mysterious place? Did Arthur belong to reality or myth? The two writers try to find the answers.*

SOMERSET MYSTERIES

SOMERSET may be part of Blake's 'green and pleasant land', but spiritually it remains a mysterious land.

Somerset is different things to different people. She defies neat easy classification. In a land so soaked in history and legend, how could it be otherwise? Historic and romantic. Impressive heights and wide landscapes. A place of solitude – and yet the scene of bitter bloody battles. Somerset is all these – and a good deal more besides.

Old Somerset, real Somerset, had sixty rivers running through it, four groups of hills – plus Sedgemoor 'with its melancholy tale of a broken dream' and glorious Exmoor. These are only some of the jewels in the crown.

Not for nothing is Somerset the Land of Arthur.

For the greater part of nine hundred years, writers and casters of spells have been telling stories about the Once and Future King. From half-forgotten history and lost legend, they have shaped one of the great epics the world has known.

Somerset and mystery go together naturally – like cider and cricket.

Mystery?

Collins English Dictionary gives us three diamond-sharp definitions: 1: an unexplained or inexplicable event, phenomenon etc; 2: a person or thing that arouses curiosity or suspense because of an unknown, obscure or enigmatic quality; 3: the state or quality of being obscure, inexplicable or enigmatic.

Somerset has another 'population'. The fact is, the landscape is peopled with ghosts.

Somerset is no place for the Doubting Thomas. There are hundreds of people, some local, others outsiders, who are convinced they have seen apparitions. Maybe in the atmosphere which is Somerset, people are more

◄ *Shadows fall across a Somerset road …*

Bossington, one of Somerset's many beautiful villages …

ready to accept a Supernatural explanation. Either way, there is a mass of evidence here for ghosts and ghostly happenings. Even if we subtract some of the claims on grounds of hallucination, there remains a solid weight of evidence.

An old spiritualist friend of mine, who died, disliked the word Supernatural. 'It should be *Supernormal*'. I have often thought of him on our journeys through Somerset – and believe he may have an important interpretation.

After a quarter of a century of investigation and study, I am coming to the view that the way to the Supernatural is through the *natural*. Doctors do not know how warts are charmed away. Specialists cannot explain how or why new tissue starts forming in a wound and stops when the wound is healed. Nobody has ever seen a wireless wave, yet it would be futile to say it does not exist.

'I think of time as a disc on a record player,' said Anthony D. Hippisley Coxe, the author of *Haunted Britain*. 'The stylus traces the present; but there is no reason why another stylus should not simultaneously pick up the music to come, or that which has passed. Our time seems to be governed by the clock; but a clock's relation to time is even less significant than that of a metre measure to the Atlantic Ocean.'

As dowsers know, different substances have different 'fields'. They are to be found in the Somerset countryside around woods and by springs. In a sentence, everything has its 'field'. Tom Lethbridge, an archaeologist who became a master dowser, progressed from finding hidden objects through dowsing to exploring the timeless world beyond death. By the time he died, he had become the 'Einstein of the paranormal'. Mr. Lethbridge believed that nature generates fields of static electricity, especially close to running water. These 'fields', he maintained, pick up and record the feelings and thoughts of people and other creatures.

If, for example, we go to a place where someone has been driven to suicide, we may experience an unpleasant atmosphere when all that is happening is the despair and death of the suicide victim is being transferred to our electrical field – in accordance with the laws of electricity.

It seems that some very powerful force impresses itself on the field – looking now on the better, brighter side of the subject, maybe the force which led to a certain place being considered 'sacred'.

Somerset somehow works on our imagination.

Back in the 1920s a writer and illustrator was travelling from North Devon to London by motor car.

Here is how Donald Maxwell reacted at one point:

'We were nearing Langport and our road ran along the ridge for the most part bordered with trees that screened the distant view. Suddenly the foliage opened out and we were looking down upon a vast plain veiled in blue and stretching mysteriously, league upon league, to the dim horizon. The lingering light of the sunset hung over the north-west and there appeared innumerable trenches or canals intersecting the flat land. These glittered in the dusk and made as eerie a scene as I have ever seen.

'We stopped and marvelled at this strange country, this unknown land so dim and dark. Bars of red cloud lay along the horizon and soon nothing was visible but the break in the evening sky and these unearthly waterways appearing as rivers of blood. The planet Mars intersected, as some say it is, with multitudinous canals, may yield such landscape as this.

'"What is it," I asked "and where are we?"

'"This is Sedgemoor," my friend replied, "the scene of the last battle in England."'

Years later, Donald Maxwell recalled the stop in this vivid dramatic way. That is the power of the place.

Some of us believe in the power of ley lines, and in Somerset we have a section of the great St. Michael line which begins at St. Michael's Mount in

Cornwall and ends on the coast north of Lowestoft. Or does it end there?

Any serious enquiry into the alignment of ancient sites must go back to 1921 – to the 30th June of that year when Alfred Watkins made a startling discovery. Watkins knew nothing of the theory of old straight tracks before it tumbled into his mind that summer afternoon. Then aged sixty-six, he had spent his early years travelling the Welsh border territory with his pony and trap as a representative for his family's milling and brewing concerns. Alfred Watkins had a natural affinity with the countryside and its people. He had other qualities too: psychic powers, sharp observation and logic.

His view of the ley system was very clear. In his book *The Old Straight Track*, published in 1925, he wrote:

'Imagine a fairy chain stretched from mountain peak to mountain peak, as far as the eye could reach, and paid out until it reached the 'high places' of the earth at a number of ridges, banks and knolls. Then visualise a mound, circular earthwork, or clump of trees, planted on these high points, and in low points in the valley other mounds ringed round with water to be seen from a distance. Then great standing stones brought to mark the way at intervals, and on a bank leading up to a mountain ridge or down to a ford, the track cut deep so as to form a guiding notch on the skyline as you come up. In a *bwlch* or mountain pass the road cuts deeply at the highest place straight through the ridge to show as a notch afar off. Here and there, at two ends of the way, a beacon fire used to lay out the track. With ponds dug on the line, or streams banked up into 'flashes' to form reflecting points on the beacon track so that it might be checked when at least once a year the beacon was fired on the traditional day. All these works exactly on the sighting line.'

Alfred Watkins may have seen the ley pattern 'in a flash' – he told his son it was like 'a flood of ancestral memory', and years of subsequent study of the subject added weight and detail to his original vision.

I have visited several locations on the St. Michael line and, as a result, agree with those who say these ley lines carry energy flows. There is usually a heightened sense of wellbeing. Our knowledge of earth energy culture stems from China where the art of divining the earth energies, flowing along the leys – dragon paths the Chinese call them – helps decision-makers select where best to build a temple or house: a location which harmonises with the flow of energy from the earth.

There are two locations in Somerset: Burrow Mump, Burrow Bridge and Glastonbury Tor. The former is a large mound, partly and perhaps totally artificial, topped by ruins – the remains of a church dedicated to St. Michael. Glastonbury Tor, with its spiral tracks winding round the hill, has a

Burrow Mump ... ▶

Supernatural look; yet these curious spiral tracks are natural and are matched by several other hillocks and tors in the county.

Anyway, my advice is go to both locations and experience for yourself. Remember the old folk believed the universe to be magical and the Earth a living creature.

KING ARTHUR?

PSYCHO-EXPANSION is a technique which enables individuals to explore and develop their sense of awareness. The claim is the mind is therefore able to move in time and space. In a sentence: it is time travel.

Personally I have not undergone psycho-expansion, but I have interviewed people in a state of regression – travelling back to an earlier life or lives. Consequently those who cannot accept reincarnation, cannot accept psycho-expansion.

I have interviewed a Westcountry housewife who claims she *was* King Arthur in a former life. She sees nothing strange or inconsistent in that once she was a man. 'Some people come back to this life many times,' she explained, 'and in very different forms . . . there seem to be no rules, save those of cause and effect.'

During these interviews I have been impressed by the variety of changes in her personality. In regression, for example, she sits differently; her voice becomes noticeably lower in key. Listening to this Aquarian lady you are aware that she is giving a kind of commentary, but no matter-of-fact commentary, no plateau of emotion. At times she is genuinely troubled, and other times highly amused. You, the interviewer, are forced to one of two conclusions: she is either a very talented actress (as far as I know she has never been on the stage) or you are watching and listening to something not quite of this world.

In March 1991, she gave me an exclusive interview for the purpose of *Somerset Mysteries*. Naturally we concentrated on Arthur's links with the county. The following is an account of that conversation.

Question: What makes you so sure that Arthur belongs to reality?

Answer: The name Arthur is really a kind of family name, a title describing a hereditary role which involves some type of leadership. I know that the Arthur who lived in the Westcountry during the period 451 A.D. to 518 A.D. belongs to my reality through my past lives research over many years.

◀ *St Michael's Tower on Glastonbury Tor ...*

The view from Glastonbury Tor ...

It was in 1979 when I first recalled this life and had no idea who he was until one group session of psycho-expansion some months later, when I was questioned while in this particular relaxed state that the technique allows. I was asked who I was and I 'heard' myself saying that I was a Celtic tribal leader giving a Celtic name which roughly translated means: 'who is of fire'. With the recall of other members of the psycho-expansion groups who did their research at different sessions we gradually discovered that many of us had been together before and lots of the information we got individually we confirmed with each other later on. So many people 'saw' me, and I 'saw' many of the others. It was quite an extraordinary time, checking this information.

Question: Do you think proof will one day emerge confirming, once and for all, that Arthur is a genuinely historical figure?

Answer: I'm not sure what sort of proof can really confirm to the general public that Arthur existed, apart from some artefact or piece of writing with his name on it! However, I'm sure that if we need some type of proof it will be revealed when the time is right. I think there will be a discovery of importance in this decade. As far as Arthur being a genuinely historical figure, I can only say that we have found this person, his family and connections operating in what is known historically as the Dark Ages in Britain with the strongest links to the Westcountry. So far, I haven't discovered him in the north and I wonder if there was another leader who was an 'Arthur' operating there at this time. The place names incorporating Arthur abound all over the country, which I find an intriguing point.

Question: Though you and I have talked about your earlier life, we've not really discussed the others. What was Merlin's influence? What kind of woman was Guinevere? What was the atmosphere of Camelot? Was Excalibur a magical sword?

Answer: Merlin's influence – or the person we will call Merlin (since one of his roles in those times was as Bishop Merlinus), was considerable. He was in fact the father of Arthur. He was a very wise man with considerable knowledge of the ancient religion, but he spent a lot of his time in travelling, particularly in Brittany where there were strong family connections. Merlin arranged for Arthur's upbringing as a warrior from a very early age with a great deal of Roman influence. He also acted as a mediator between the tribes, bringing them together in order that there should be more of a united front when the invasions began to develop more seriously. He advised Arthur on many matters – sometimes with difficulty – since Arthur was a bit headstrong, especially in his younger years.

Ploughing through the ages

Guinevere – the name was rather different then – was betrothed to Arthur when he was very young, around the age of fifteen or sixteen when he went through a ceremony in Brittany where there was a great gathering of tribes at Carnac. Attached to this ceremony was his taking on some formal kind of responsibility as a leader – a dedication I think.

I'm not quite sure how Guinevere fits into my recall, except she didn't return to Britain with Arthur at that time. This was an arranged betrothal as so many seemed to be in those times, to establish the links with family and tribes. There seemed to be a lot of inter-marrying and everyone seemed quite happy with these arrangements. I 'remember' her as having very fair hair – just a girl – but from an important family. She had a child, a son, and they came to Dorset first and then Somerset when the boy was about two years old.

I am not sure about Camelot. The word never brings me any 'far memory'. However, if I 'ask' about Cadbury Castle I get an immediate response as being a very important place for Arthur which he used as a great fortress having caused it to be strengthened and developed to contain whole tribes. I have never visited it in this life so far except through 'mind' research. This reveals a strong ley line connecting it with Glastonbury which seems to continue up and around into the Severn area and the Forest of Dean where Arthur also had connections. The name Caerleon also gives me a very strong reaction.

The sword Excalibur I discovered was a very special sword which manifested at Avebury. When I was doing this piece of research, I was quite amazed and reluctant to give the details of what happened – it's far too much like something out of a film! However, suffice it to say that I now understand that Excalibur is a symbol of great strength and protection which may appear to anyone – perhaps in meditation, where there is a particularly strong need which involves mankind.

Question: Can you give us a word picture of the Somerset of your day?

Answer: The Somerset of Arthur's day was extremely beautiful – such forests of trees . . . There seemed to be a great deal more water, first of all coming in on the sea coast not far from Minehead and of course all around Glastonbury Tor. During this lifetime of Arthur I seemed to be mainly travelling on two routes – one was all along the northern coasts of the Westcountry and the other was into Dorset. I think Somerset was really the centre of Arthur's activities, or perhaps he always seemed to be returning there. It was such a fragrant area – or perhaps the senses were more sharp in the people of those times. What always struck me when 'mind travelling' were the great number of trees everywhere.

Question: Elsewhere in this book, I have put the question to some people: 'Why is Somerset such a mysterious place?' I now put that question to you, as Arthur, and I put the same question to you as you are in 1991. It's interesting that you spent part of this life living in Somerset.

Answer: I wonder if Arthur thought that Somerset was a mysterious place. He was certainly aware that it was served by a great ley line and that Glastonbury was a very 'energised' place. By this I mean that the force field in the vicinity of the Tor was exceptional – it was enhanced. This effect draws one back to a place because the atmosphere is rarified – an excellent healing centre. He had occasion to seek help there for many of his wounds sustained in battle.

Now, in the 1990s I still think that Somerset has an air of mystery about it, but like most counties you have to get off the main roads to 'feel' it. When I lived in Somerset as a child just before the 1950s I was fortunate in having the opportunity to accompany my father in his car when he had to visit many farms in the course of his work. Looking back, I'm so glad to have experienced those journeys by road and lane with little traffic about, and to be able to explore the country churches. It truly is a county of many contrasts with its levels and great protecting hills. We had moved from Surrey and my lasting memory of Somerset is always as the county of the meadowsweet growing in great clumps everywhere, but especially heady and fragrant near the canals. For all our outings around the country places the one place my father and I never visited was Glastonbury!

So, I had no preconceived ideas about this area when in 1979 – over thirty years later I was exploring it through the technique of psycho-expansion and mind travel and making notes of my findings and feelings as a tribal leader in the fifth century A.D. I finally got there in the 1980s in this life and found it difficult to cope with the different layers of occupation since Celtic times. I have still not climbed the Tor itself, yet I can very easily go back to being in Arthur's body and recall the view. I must return just for old times' sake!

Question: I think you, as you are now, had a strange experience in Somerset. Can you tell me about it?

Answer: In 1984, my eldest daughter was married and she and her husband moved to a house near Williton, Somerset. A year later, I was visiting them and unfortunately strained my back. Sitting in her living room, I could see the church tower on the horizon and my intuition moved me (very gingerly!) to get into my car to discover the reason why I must go. On arrival, I explored the church – St. Decuman's – which was very well kept – and then the grounds, where I found a little path sloping down to a garden and, I think, a well. This garden had been lovingly created out of a wilderness, I believe, but the sense of peace within it suddenly overwhelmed me. Then I felt a strong line of energy behind me as I descended the path with halting steps – due to my back condition. I stepped sideways and found it less

distinguishable, so I positioned myself again and stood still allowing my back to be against the flow. Some ten minutes later, I turned to climb back up the garden path with the realisation that my steps were now unfaltering – there was only the slightest twinge in my back!

I reached my car and this time there was no need to ease myself into the driving seat and when I returned to my daughter demonstrating how much better my back was, all she said was, "You're mad, mother!" At that time, as you will have gathered, she was not 'into all that stuff', her own words for that which isn't obvious! She has since learned differently for herself which is important. Learning about your intuition and ultimately trusting it is probably the most important step in self-discovery. Anyway, I went on to enjoy the rest of my stay thanks to my intuition and Mother Earth's healing energies. Others may wonder if St. Decuman had a hand in it!

Question: Finally, as you believe in reincarnation, do you think Arthur will reappear one day in his Arthurian form?

Answer: For me, reincarnation appears to be obvious due to my own experiences of past lives and many years of other research, so when you ask me if I think Arthur will reappear one day in his Arthurian form I can only reply by saying that if he did, would he be recognised? The Arthur that I found myself to be as a tribal leader in the Fifth century was only a part of an intricate story which somehow captured the headlines of the day as an idea and was passed on through myth and legend to describe the journey that man undertakes through a physical life. The story and the idea still survive because the pitfalls, the decisions, the courageous acts and the romances are what we all experience in a lifetime. We all have a quest whether it be in a material sense or a spiritual one – it just depends on how enquiring your nature is and what your intent, as well as how your inner needs must be met. So I believe we are all Arthurs, or part of his idea right now, whether we are men, women or children.

The discovery of my own incarnations has led me to understand that a soul may be called on at any time to fulfill a particular leadership role. My own role as the fifth century Arthur was certainly in defending his people at a critical time, but it was his love of the land in which he found himself operating that was important to him. We face a similar threat now, but on a global scale. Our desire for swift evolution has polluted the land which supports us – the planet Earth – so *we* have become our own worst enemies.

Will Arthur reappear in his Arthurian form? I think he already has – in each one of us. How must we Arthurs respond in saving our lands, our planet? Many of the answers lie hidden in myth and legend.'

Withies …

HAUNTED SOMERSET

THE GHOSTS of Somerset are various and numerous.

Many of them 'inhabit' ancient locations like churches and hostelries. Old buildings have often been scarred by history. If we take churches, for example, centuries of prayers have been offered up within their walls. There is also a school of thought, that many of our churches stand on former pagan sites *and* on ley lines – all of which could increase their potential for Supernatural manifestation. Or if we consider inns of the county, there are centuries of living and enjoyment associated with these convivial places.

Some psychic investigators also believe there is a connection between ghosts and stone. They believe that, in some curious way, the stone can somehow absorb 'emanations' from people, especially in stressful times, and store them as we might store vision on film or sound on tape. From occasion to occasion that stored 'information' is replayed – all of which gets us back to why when we enter an old building we may get an impression of happiness – or depression.

I have always been interested in the fact that the majority of British ghosts are phantom ladies. This may not be surprising when we discover that statistically there are fewer men in Britain – and always have been. I have another theory. Having interviewed more than three hundred and fifty people claiming Supernatural experience, I know the majority are women. Men fearing scorn and ridicule perhaps?

Somerset certainly has her share of 'ladies'.

The Theatre Royal at Bath has a Grey Lady who occasionally sits in a box above the audience – some say she threw herself to her death. Then at Crowcombe there have been reports of a 'lady in blue' seen in the Rectory. In *Ghosts of Somerset* Peter Underwood has written an account of a ghostly female encountered at Porlock: nothing vague or misty. She was 'in evening dress: a gleaming white silk gown, patterned with dark spots; her head was bare, and her shoulder – curls fell over a falling lace collar. She was very beautiful.'

20

Ancient pollarded willows

There have been accounts too of phantom white ladies seen standing guard over bridges and trackways. The White Lady of Wellow though was no guardian spirit, for it was said her rare appearance was supposed to 'announce' a death in the Hungerford family.

Witches too punctuate Somerset history. One such character Jane Brooks, who hailed from Shepton Mallet, bewitched a twelve-year-old boy by offering him 'a bite of a magical apple.' The unfortunate lad immediately became airborne, finally crashlanding on the doorstep of a house. Jane Brooks was charged with witchcraft, found guilty and duly hanged at Chard.

In 1680 a man was tried at Taunton Assizes for witchcraft and acquitted by a sympathetic judge. Suddenly an old woman cried out from the courtroom: 'God bless your Lordship! . . . Forty years ago they would have hanged me for a witch and they could not, and now they would have hanged my poor son'.

Here in the Westcountry we are in Celtic territory where the worship of the spirits of water once held great significance. Pins were dropped into wells – unspoken wishes made. Time was when there were two types of well: the wishing well and the cursing well. The latter were much in evidence until the early 1800s when they were filled in after being regarded as 'unsavoury relics of pagan superstition.'

Against this kind of background Somerset is natural ghost hunting country, but I must not give the impression of all local ghosts being wicked – or even frightening. Indeed some of the Somerset sightings have been so solid, so life-like, that the realization has only struck the observer later – say when the figure has inexplicably vanished. Discovering the identity of a ghost, of course, can be an interesting challenge. For instance the ghost of Forde Abbey, south-west of Chard, is thought to be that of Thomas Chard who was Abbot of the Cistercian establishment at the Dissolution. When the ghost has been observed there, he is normally standing by the table in the great hall, gazing about the place he loved in his lifetime.

The identity of 'the Spanish traveller' murdered at the Plough Hotel, Holford in 1555, however, remains a mystery. Was he a spy? Was a rich traveller killed for his money? Who was he? We shall never know the answers but James Westworth Day and Peter Underwood, two eminent ghost writers and hunters, have written of 'a dark cloaked figure' seen at The Plough.

The only seance in which I have taken part was during the early hours of a Saturday morning in Somerset, when the circle endeavoured to make contact with a ghost in a haunted house. As it was at a private residence, and we all agreed on secrecy, I cannot give details, but it was a fascinating experience.

Thoughtful Felicity Young in her fascinating *Curiosities of Exmoor* devoted a chapter to Haunted Exmoor: 'This sense of mystery and the Supernatural is not merely an echo from a distant past or secondhand experience, the impression continues to this very day . . . Exmoor can boast a rich variety of hauntings – black dogs on the moor, rattling chains, several sightings of sad figures with tragic pasts.'

Felicity is correct about the range of Somerset hauntings, theirs is an extraordinary diversity. A ghostly funeral procession of Quakers has been seen at Catcott, near Bridgwater. Bad omen lights have been observed at Shapwick near Glastonbury. Inexplicably mature stags have been present at more than one Exmoor funeral, and phantom trains have travelled along a railway track closed for more than three decades!

On Hallowe'en morning 1990 I did a ghost phone-in for Radio Cornwall with presenter Tamsin Thomas. We were looking for listeners with genuine ghost stories, and the last caller on the programme was a lady called Anne.

This is how the programme ended:

Tamsin Thomas: 'Tell me about your story.'

Anne: 'It was several years ago, my husband and I were coming home from the Severn Valley Railway, and we decided to pop into Glastonbury Abbey. It was fairly late and we couldn't take one of those tapes with us to tell us about the Abbey, so we just went around for a walk. At the time we had our dog with us. We walked around the Abbey and my husband said "Let's go up towards the high altar to have a close look at that." We went up towards the high altar, and all of a sudden my dog started growling and I thought: "What are you doing? Stop growling." But he wouldn't stop and we went a bit further towards the high altar, and he literally stopped dead and tried to go backwards, and he wouldn't stop growling, so we thought we'd better take him away just in case he's not happy. And we walked away, but I thought "Well, there must have been something there." So we took him back again, but he did exactly the same thing again. Now we don't know why he did it or what was there. We didn't see anything, but he *knew* there was somebody there.'

Tamsin Thomas: 'Goes back to what we were saying about dogs again doesn't it, Michael, and their intuition?'

Michael Williams: 'Yes, very interesting that here is another dog case, and I've certainly had two very vivid Supernatural experiences with dogs.'

Tamsin Thomas: 'It's obvious that dogs tune into these things quicker than humans.'

Michael Williams: 'I think that's so, and Glastonbury has a very haunted reputation.'

Anne: 'Yes, they reckon that King Arthur is buried there, I wouldn't have thought that he'd been buried under the high altar, but whatever it was the dog sensed it.'

Michael Williams: 'I don't think it necessarily had anything to do with Arthur at all. A member of the Ghost Club some years ago thought he was seeing a group of religious people touring the area, and he thought they were going to see some gathering in a part of the Abbey and followed them. Then when he got there the place was empty. Not a soul to be seen. So it's that type of place. I don't say it happens every day but, as I was saying earlier, time is like a film and when it gets tangled or twisted we pick up fragments of other times, and I think your dog picked up another time.'

Above, storms gather over Glastonbury. Below, a facet of Somerset's farming landscape.

THE MYSTERY OF MYTH AND LEGEND

'IT IS A riddle wrapped in a mystery inside an enigma.'

That was Sir Winston Churchill talking about Russia in a BBC radio broadcast on the first day of October 1939.

Such words could apply to Somerset within the context of myth and legend, for Somerset is truly a land of legend. Though, of course, legend and myth are two different things.

Myth is basically about gods and superhuman beings of an earlier age. Myth has existed in society across the centuries. Myths are essentially serious stories reflecting a society's spiritual foundations. Indeed they would seem to be a basic constituent of human culture. Moreover they impart a feeling of awe for whatever is mysterious and marvellous in life.

Some of us believe myths address the fundamental, the important questions which all thinking people still ask. Who am I? What is the nature of the universe? How can I lead a satisfying life? How do I reconcile myself to the thing we call death?

Myths were originally created as entertaining stories with a serious purpose. Their wide appeal and fascination have enabled some of them to survive for hundreds and sometimes thousands of years.

Legend, in contrast, is a tale thought to have historical basis – as in the case of Robin Hood. Folktales are a kind of cousin: a subdivision of myth. A certain overlapping is inevitable. Folktales are the oldest and purest examples of the storyteller's art, but a folktale, at its best, is not to be underestimated.

It can be an illumination concerning the nature of things, setting men and women in a frame with the animals and the plants, the world and weather, and often the other world of the Supernatural.

Some writers go to the heart of the matter on their opening page. Sally Jones did so in her excellent *Legends of Somerset*, when she opened with these words:

'The legends of Somerset are like a game of 'Chinese Whispers' played long ago. First comes the original story, whether a domestic tragedy like Walford's murder of his pathetic half-witted wife, a great historical event like the Battle of Sedgemoor, or the coming of Joseph of Arimathea as tin-trader and missionary.

'Over the years, the stories gradually acquire a deeper resonance as the echoes of the original event, far from dying down, continue to rumble and reverberate. The tale is passed on with subtle additions and distortions. Real life being necessarily full of *non sequiturs* and loose ends, the tale-tellers frequently prefer to tie them up with a dramatic flourish, an element of fantasy or even a rustic joke.'

When we think or talk of Jesus Christ, we come to the biggest mystery of all: God in human form, triumphing over the thing we call death and proving the reality of eternal life. That has been the belief and conviction of millions of men and women, within the framework of the Christian faith, for a span of all but two thousand years.

Did Christ physically come to Somerset?

There is a legend, bordering on a mixture of hope and belief, that the young Jesus did precisely that. It is believed Joseph was an uncle of Mary, the mother of Jesus. Joseph was more than a wealthy trader and merchant, he was a skilful sailor and navigator. So it was natural he should suggest the boy Jesus should come with him on one of his voyages. And, of course, it is historically feasible.

After all, Blake, the mystic, wrote those stirring words:

> *And did those Feet in ancient time*
> *Walk upon England's mountain green*
> *And was the Holy Lamb of God*
> *On England's pleasant pastures seen?*

Arthur inevitably looms larger than life in Somerset folklore. One contributor to these pages, of course, insists he belongs to reality. That may be so. Certainly over the years Arthur, in the eyes and thinking of many students, has advanced from a mythical figure into an historical possibility, even probability.

The debate about the reality of Arthur will rumble on, yet curiously his myth lives on in a quite remarkable way, working a strange wonder in men and women, boys and girls from different lands and different cultures: all touched by the art, the history and the literature. The heritage may be ours, but the magic undeniably belongs to Arthur.

As a boy I read and enjoyed R.D. Blackmore's *Lorna Doone*. I enjoyed it even more as a radio series – in those days we called it 'the wireless'. Then I assumed the Doones were fictional characters created by the vivid imagi-

The Glastonbury Thorn, one of the most enduring of Somerset legends ...

nation of Mr Blackmore. It was nearly forty years later when I discovered this was probably not the case.

Ronald Duncan knew Exmoor well. Ezra Pound called him 'the lone wolf of English letters.' He lived, farmed and wrote at his home high on the north coast of Devon. Writing to me from there back in 1976 Ronald had this to say on the subject:

'Ever since *Lorna Doone* was published in 1869, Exmoor has been known as Doone country. For years I thought this was an interesting example of where an author's tale had, by being identified with a particular place, created a legend. Generally the reverse process obtains, and the legend gives rise to the story. But in this case I find there is considerable evidence to suggest that Blackmore did base his story on fact.

'It was obviously true that the moors had always been the favourite haunt of outlaws, and some of the more notorious hunting parsons and ruffianly squires lived there. But in 1901 a lady calling herself Ida M. Browne or Audrey Doon wrote an article in the *West Somerset Free Press* which shed light on this subject. She claimed to have been of the original Doone family, and stated that Sir Ensor Doone, the robber chief of Blackmore's story, was the twin brother of the Earl of Moray, who was banished from Doune Castle near Stirling in Perthshire as a result of a family feud. After vainly seeking redress in London, he decided to abandon land and fortune, and turning his face to the setting sun journeyed thirteen days westwards with his wife and one servant, until he reached a ruined farmhouse in the East Lyn valley, not far from Oare Ford, and decided to settle there.

Miss Doon in her article quoted from a diary kept by a member of the family in the eighteenth century which contained the following entries:

'1747 Sept 3rd. Went to Barum on my way to the place they called Oare, whence our people came after their cruel treatment by the Earl Moray.

Sept 7th. Got to Oare and then to the valley of the Lyn. The scenery very bonny like

Water flows gently through the low land of Somerset

28

our own land but the part extremely wild and lonely. Wandered about and thought of the old days of the family there, which I gathered were not peaceable.'

In travelling through the folklore of Somerset more than once I recalled the words of the American writer, the late Truman Capote, who, prefacing various pieces of writing put into book form under the title of *The Dogs Bark*, wrote:

'Everything herein is factual, which doesn't mean that it is the truth, but it is as nearly so as I can make it. Journalism, however, can never be altogether pure – nor can the camera, for after all, art is not distilled water: personal perceptions, prejudices, one's sense of selectivity pollute the purity of germless truth.'

In Somerset you cannot escape legends and you cannot begin to understand Somerset without reference to them and related folklore and myth. Without them, vital pieces are missing from the jigsaw puzzle that is Somerset and its past.

The enigma deepens too in that some real Somerset characters acquire a legendary quality. History and personalities cover this lovely varied landscape. Sir Bevil Grenville fell in the hour of victory on the hills above Bath. The celebrated fighting Hoods of Nelson's band of brothers came from Butleigh and Cricket St. Thomas. The great actor Sir Henry Irving hailed from Keinton Mandeville, and, deeper back in time, comes that shadowy figure of 'one of the most marvellous men of the medieval days'. Roger Bacon first saw the light of day in the old town of Ilchester. And if we come forward to this century we must not forget Rollo John Oliver Meyer, the man who created Millfield School and captained Somerset at cricket. 'Boss', they called him. A remarkable man, he encouraged princes to pay more for their sons to go to Millfield to subsidise the children of the poor.

In Somerset the dividing lines often grow blurred. Fact or fiction? Past or present? And herein lies much of the mystery and magic.

WHY?

AT THIS POINT on our exploration I decided to pose the question: 'Why is Somerset such a mysterious place?'

First, I talked with Felicity Young, the author of *Curiosities of Exmoor*. Felicity, who lived in Somerset for twenty years, now resides at Tintagel high on the coast of North Cornwall, where she leads a very full life. A member of the British Horse Society, she is a riding instructor at the Tall Trees Stables, just outside Camelford, on the edge of Bodmin Moor. She teaches yoga and paints water colours. Since 1984 she has contributed more than two hundred and fifty illustrations for a whole range of Bossiney titles – some of which appear inside these pages. She has also written a chapter on Lawrence of Arabia in *Dorset Mysteries* and, more recently, in *Strange Dorset Stories* a chapter on Charlotte Bryant, a small-time prostitute who was hanged for the murder of her husband.

In *Curiosities of Exmoor* Felicity Young opened her first page with these words: 'Exmoor itself is a Curiosity.'

Now I asked her what made Somerset such a landscape of mystery.

'I am sure that each person you ask will come up with a different answer depending on where their interests lie,' she said. 'For me I think the mystery of Somerset can be found in its areas of wild unspoilt countryside. There are several distinct pockets of land, such as the levels of Sedgemoor, the bracken-covered Quantocks, the Blackdown Hills and, of course, Exmoor, all of which have their own unique atmosphere. When anyone talks of Somerset, Exmoor immediately springs to *my* mind. It is definitely my favourite part of the country. There are many legends and plenty of ancient history spread throughout Somerset but Exmoor exudes a different kind of mystery. When you are there, you can't help but sense that you have walked into a different world. The remoter parts remain untamed, lacking in human habitation, there are signs of settlement belonging to early man, as far back as the Stone Age . . . but modern man has relinquished the land to Mother Nature. You enter a time warp when you venture into the heart of Exmoor.

Felicity Young, who lived in Somerset for twenty years and still makes regular visits to the county

'Mystery lurks around each corner, in each wooded valley and over the brow of every hill, a wonderful place. As a keen horse rider I find open spaces exhilarating and Exmoor certainly has plenty of space. It offers a challenge, to gallop across the heather and bracken, but one is always aware that Exmoor is full of surprises, full of mystery – deep bogs which can swallow up an animal. Who knows what might lie beneath the surface in these places? There are areas of dense unexplored woodland and up on the high moor are the magnificent red deer running wild with the Exmoor ponies.

Acora, the gifted Romany clairvoyant, who comes to Bridgwater Fair each year.

The secret places of Exmoor ...

The weather can be atrocious, the thick mists rolling across the hills, obscuring the landscape, a cold biting wind chilling you to the bone, but still it draws you like a magnet. Even on a bright sunny day in summer there is an eeriness lingering on. Mystery surrounds every aspect of this beautiful piece of Somerset. Time stands still on Exmoor.'

Next I talked with Acora, the gifted Romany clairvoyant who has been called 'Prince of the Soothsayers.' A Scorpio subject, Acora comes from a long line of travelling people.

'My clairvoyancy has not been learnt from books or teachers. It's something inherited through blood and birth.' This remarkable character had next to no schooling, and even today he confesses: 'I prefer to read palms than words in a book!' Yet his predictions have won newspaper headlines and earned him T.V. and radio broadcasts all over the Westcountry.

Though Devon-born and Cornwall-based, Acora makes regular visits to Somerset.

'I go to Bridgwater Fair every year,' he told me, 'and whatever the weather there are always lots of people wanting consultations, wanting me to look into the future for them. We Romanies call it 'dukkering' . . . looking ahead, making predictions . . . well, there are a lot of 'dukkering-minded' people in Somerset. Like you, I feel there's a strong something in Somerset; maybe it's all wrapped up in its long history and the fact that you have these long established Somerset families. You go into a churchyard and you'll see the same names cropping up on the headstones going back hundreds of years.'

Acora, who started making forecasts at the age of seven, sees parallels: 'Somerset and Cornwall . . . the two places have a lot in common. There's a lot of superstition in Cornwall; there's a lot of superstition in Somerset. You go to some of these smaller Cornish and Somerset villages and, in some ways, you're stepping back in time. But if you go the other way, and cross the Somerset border and go into a place like Bristol you're in another world: all modern and no real Supernatural feelings.

'I'm not surprised to hear that Somerset has loads of ghosts. It's that kind of place . . . you've got all these old buildings. You've got Somerset cider – now that's another kind of spirit! – but even with cider you've got these old country traditions. There's this strong sense of the past and what a past . . . all those battles, witchcraft and hangings, the tales of King Arthur. All that may belong to the long ago but somehow something lingers on.'

My third interviewee was Rosemary Clinch who is a psychic all-rounder: numerologist and dowser, she also practises *I Ching*. A strong contributor to the Somerset and Avon side of our Bossiney list, her titles include *Supernatural in Somerset* and *Curious Bristol*. She is the co-author of *King Arthur in Somerset* and *Unknown Somerset*. Rosemary has made a number of local radio broadcasts and is becoming widely known as a lecturer on a variety of Supernatural subjects.

In *Supernatural in Somerset* she has written: 'Somerset as much as any county has its share of the Supernatural, ghosts, poltergeists and people who have had strange experiences or gifts which are part of the paranormal . . . Somerset has always had some special kind of magic for me.'

I put the question to her, and standing on Mendip looking out over the Vale of Avalon, this was her response:

'Many reasons come to mind but mainly I feel it is its holistic nature. I mean, just look at it, the wonderful variety, the hills, pastureland, wetland, and sand and sea. I am constantly aware the Somerset landscape is composed of many features found in other counties and this makes me sense there must be a special reason for its existence. To me it resembles a keepsake. I see it as samples taken from the vast design of our country which has been blended in a final flourish to become Somerset, yet, in some mysterious way, holding an essential purpose for mankind.

'Somerset has become essential to me. I was not born here but as a child, school visits to Cheddar Gorge left the seed of a love I was to know. Growth is what life is all about, in mind, body and spirit and it is here I feel I am making the most progress in many ways.

Psychic all-rounder Rosemary Clinch, author of Supernatural in Somerset. ▶

'Atmosphere is important. It is strong in Somerset for creating the perfect setting when viewing the past and the present, but it also gives some a glimpse into the future. You see, atmosphere may enhance history and legend but many people, including visitors, have told me of experiencing déjà vu, a sense of belonging and knowing they will return. People have their special places and mine is here on Mendip. It helps me to recharge, clear my mind and think clearly before moving on. I often sit here admiring the contours of the Mendip ridge running to the sea.

'It reminds me of the ancient Chinese art of geomancy, the deliberate reshaping of the land which is said to enhance the vital forces of the earth for benefit. I cannot see north Somerset remaining with Avon County for long. Sooner or later it will return, drawn by the magnetic forces of nature's own essential plan I mentioned previously.

'Talking about north Somerset, I did have in Clevedon what I believe can only be a ghostly experience. I was on a photographic sortie, my first location Lady Bay. It was early morning and the atmosphere terrific with a calm sea and the sun shrouded through a sea mist. On the way down the path from the road to the beach I met a robin who kept me company. The beach was deserted except for a picturesque piece of driftwood. The robin watched me taking my pictures and then we returned together back up the path until we reached the bush where we had first met. A few feet away, not far from the top of the path and the road, another path crossed, and while saying goodbye to my little friend, suddenly, out of the corner of my eye I saw someone jogging by. Slightly embarrassed at being caught out deep in conversation with a bird, I turned to see the person fully but no-one was there. My view of the path and to the road was clear so where could he have gone? I questioned two fishermen who appeared on the path, walking in the same direction as the jogger, but they had seen no-one. Alone again, I resumed my conversation with my little friend, feeling somehow it was far from strange to talk to the birds!'

Finally, I talked with Peter Underwood, President of the Ghost Club, the man rated 'Britain's No. 1 ghost hunter.' Peter is another strong contributor to the Bossiney list. He has written *Ghosts of Somerset* and companion titles on hauntings in Cornwall, Devon, Dorset and Wiltshire. Bossiney has also published his *Mysterious Places* and *Westcountry Hauntings*.

There is no man – alive or dead – better qualified to comment on the ghostly character of Somerset:

'Somerset can provide exciting examples of practically every kind of paranormal activity known to psychical researchers, be it a screaming skull, traditional and historical phantoms, poltergeistry, modern ghosts, crisis apparitions, atmospheric photograph ghosts, earthbound spirits, cyclic activity, evidence of survival, family ghosts, haunted objects and many instances of

Peter Underwood, president of the Ghost Club.

current ghostly activity. There is also a remarkable instance of a vanishing house, recounted to me by no less a person than the distinguished authority on folklore, Christina Hole.

'But why? A belief in ghosts is as old as the human race; man has always refused to accept that the death of the physical body means annihilation and clings to the belief that 'something', the 'soul' perhaps, lives on and under certain conditions that we have not yet fully understood it is occasionally possible for a personality in another world than this to return and be recognized. The scientific fraternity is being increasingly forced to accept that the evidence for paranormal activity is overwhelming.

'Somerset is full of legend, it is rich territory for psychical investigation but exactly why that should be so I cannot say with any certainty. Perhaps it has something to do with the romantic and historic million acres that is Somerset; something to do with the vast landscapes and the impressive heights; something to do with the deep solitude to be found here in this sacred soil . . . Somerset is a secret and a special place.'

SOME SOMERSET CRIME

MURDER is usually a mysterious affair. The motive driving a man or woman to kill is invariably complex, and here in idyllic Somerset the complexity is even deeper: peaceful countryside and yet often the setting for vicious crime.

In a way Somerset is something of a 'rogues gallery'.

But the Westcountry has had no killers to compare with the really notorious murderers of British crime – nobody in the bloody league of Burke and Hare, Crippen, Charlie Peace and, more recently, the Yorkshire Ripper.

Oddly enough though, the other Ripper, Jack the Ripper, who killed five London prostitutes in the autumn of 1888 may have been a Westcountryman: Montague John Druitt, a son of Dorset, who lies buried in Wimborne cemetery. My co-author in her splendid tour across legendary Dorset in factual mood has written: 'The truth behind the awful murders may never be known. All the investigations by criminologists over the years have failed to produce conclusive proof. But Druitt was certainly one of the most likely suspects.'

Somerset's past is undeniably littered with corpses, victims of 'murder most foul'.

There was John Walford, who was condemned to rot after being hanged at the very spot where he had killed his wife. Albert Pierrepoint, Britain's final professional hangman, did some of his work at Shepton Mallet. And, deeper back in time, we must not forget the Hang Fair Days at Ilchester. Until the early 1800s hangings took place just outside Ilchester on land called Gallows Five Acres. Big crowds attended and Hang Fair Days helped to boost the economy in this corner of Somerset.

The case concerning John Walford, a young Somerset charcoal burner, is especially sad. He dearly loved a girl called Ann Rice, but his lonely, remote occupation led him to marrying a slut called Jenny. She hung around his hut, and ultimately became pregnant. Their marriage lasted just seventeen days, and the Judge, Lord Kenyon, wept as he sentenced the young man to

'…in idyllic Somerset the complexity is even deeper…'

a revolting earthly end: hanged first by the neck until he was dead and then in a cage, for all Somerset to see, for a calendar month and one day.

The Westcountry too has had more than its share of crime connected with incest. A case that happened in the year 1933, might have happened in 1833. Morse, who resided at Curry Mallett, went for an afternoon walk with his twelve-year-old niece Dorothy Brewer. Later that afternoon in a heavy storm he returned home *alone*. Morse said he had left Dorothy sitting by a river while he went to look at some rabbit traps – and that she was no longer there when he came back to the river bank. He somehow hinted Dorothy might have committed suicide.

The police found her body – her stomach containing an astonishing quantity of rum – moreover, further enquiry showed the little girl was pregnant. Deeper enquiry revealed that Morse was probably her father.

Challenged, Morse admitted incest, but said the girl had agreed to a sui-

An artist's impression by Paul Honeywill of William Thornton

cide pact. Then he made the mistake of switching his story, saying he had found her drowned when he returned from inspecting the traps. The police probed deeper and discovered Dorothy was, in fact, Morse's daughter, his sister her mother.

Earlier there had been a wicked child murder on Exmoor: in the 1850s seven-year-old Anna Burgess was murdered by her father, and but for the Sherlock Holmes-like efforts of William Thornton, clerk in Holy Orders, it might have remained an unsolved Somerset mystery.

The late Jack Hurley, who was an authority on Somerset matters, told me there was an odd sequel to the Burgess business. Another scoundrel of a father was lodging at Simonsbath with his young daughter and there had been local whispers of 'another Burgess'. It was Mrs Thornton who warned her husband of the possibility of a second child murder. Thornton went to the father and 'bought' the six-year-old child. It was agreed the father should pay the Thorntons the sum of two shillings and six pence weekly, and, in return, they would clothe, feed, board and educate the girl until she was mature enough to venture into the world of adults.

Who knows but that Mrs Thornton's intuition may have averted a second Exmoor child murder?

I suppose my interest in murder dates from an early age and relates to cricket. I was scoring for Cornwall, and, at lunch, sat next to a young Cornish cricketer called Miles Giffard. Little did I realize that one day

The view from Walford's Gibbet

41

Miles Giffard would batter his parents to death and wheelbarrow them over a Cornish cliff.

A while back Acora touched on the affinities between Somerset and Cornwall and, curiously, they have certain parallels in the field of murder: a surprisingly high number of killings have taken place in both, often at odd hours and in queer places.

The mentality of the murderer is a murky place. There was Neville Heath with his murderous diamond weave whip. Before Heath went to the scaffold, he asked for a Scotch, and when they agreed he said: 'I think I'll make it a double!'.

But getting back specifically to Somerset, it's an interesting fact that there has been relatively little unsolved major crime in the past – a tribute to Somerset's bush-telegraph? Fifty years ago, in the rural areas everybody knew everybody else. Today there is a less 'local' population and, with fast cars and fast motorways, a criminal may stand a better chance of getting away from the scene of *his* crime.

The great majority of Somerset murders have been committed by men, but there have been women killers. The last woman to be burnt in Somerset was Mary Norwood who poisoned her husband in 1765. First, they strangled her, and then placed her on the fire. It was not until near the end of the eighteenth century that women were hanged, the same as men. Again Somerset played an historic part in that the man who pioneered the new legislation was none other than Sir Benjamin Hammet, M.P. for Taunton.

Then there were the sex crimes of the Victorian reign. Again Somerset had its share – like the murder of milkmaid Eliza Pain which took place at Worle. Charlie Wakeley and his girlfriend Eliza went for an evening stroll. They lay down in a ditch to embrace. At a certain point, Eliza gripped Charlie's wrists and said 'No!'; but Charlie, in a state of great excitement, produced his pocket knife and cut the girl's throat. Incredibly Eliza managed to run into the road, falling at the feet of a passerby. Charlie groaned 'I must die!' – and so he did on the scaffold of Bristol gaol.

Studying just some of Somerset's various deaths, I recall a man who knew the Exmoor acres of Somerset so well. Farmer and poet, playwright and autobiographer, short story writer and film critic Ronald Duncan was a man of various parts. In an early and long out of print Bossiney title *Facets of Crime*, he thoughtfully reflected:

'Though I do not read thrillers, I do follow the reports of criminal proceedings. It was Yeats who encouraged me in this pursuit when he wrote to me just before he died and advised me as a young dramatist to read *The News of the World* instead of *The Times*. Glancing through such court cases, I have generally found my sympathy engaged on the side of the prisoner.

'There, but for the grace of God, etc.' Surely, any honest man – that is, a man who does not steal from himself – must admit that it is *accident* and not virtue which keeps him out of the dock? If this is so, then this collection of criminal cases is a part of any man's biography; reading them we learn something about the criminal who is ourself at one remove.

Like hunger, thirst and sex, crime is one of the few human attributes which is completely universal. It is even more universal than Art itself. Nations and races can differ in their literature, language and religious beliefs or politics, but these differences are essentially superficial compared with man's basic nature. It is crime alone which stamps us as all belonging to mankind.'

Idyllic Somerset

CREATIVITY – AND MYSTERY

TWO OF the really mysterious elements about Somerset are how it has fired creativity – and has drawn creative characters like a magnet.

In July 1983 author and journalist Bel Mooney told *The Western Daily Press* how an impulsive move to buy an old rectory in the village of Upper Swainswick changed her life – and that of her husband, broadcaster Jonathan Dimbleby.

'You change when you move to the country, and it is certainly true of me. It is one of the reasons why I feel so very *grateful* to this village – it has improved me. I came here to find peace, and to bring the children up surrounded by beauty. The unexpected benefit came with my own work.

'I know for a fact that I would never have become a novelist (and I have just started the second one) without the contemplative inspiration of this valley, and my happiness here.'

Then if we head for another part of Somerset: Exmoor and Porlock in particular, we discover an interesting link with the West End theatre. That timeless composer Vivian Ellis made Porlock his beautiful retreat for something like half a century, often spending half the year here.

Back in the early 1980s he told my old friend and fellow Bossiney author David Foot:

'Do you realise I wrote the whole of *Bless The Bride* down there? C.B. Cochran came to discuss it and was taken out for a ride along the beautiful coastal road by my sister. And all he could talk about was the Messel scenery for the show!

'I like to live in a very simple manner in my Porlock cottage. I've got an old upright piano and that is where so many of my pieces have been composed.

'In the first place, though, I usually sit in bed and write on an old pastry board. I can envisage the whole concept best that way. Then I start to try things out on the piano.

Coleridge Cottage ...

'With me there's a little inspiration and a lot of hard work.'

Bestselling author Leslie Thomas is another with a Somerset connection; the author of *The Virgin Soldiers* lived for a while at Somerton. Satirist, broadcaster and raconteur Ned Sherrin and his happy childhood memories at Kingweston – Sir Hugh Casson and his six years as Bath's consultant architect: Somerset has a distinguished catalogue.

One of the most eminent cricket writers today is a son of Somerset, David Foot, who hails from East Coker – T.S. Eliot's East Coker. He has produced a string of fine books, notably *Harold Gimblett, Tormented Genius of Cricket*, of which the great John Arlott wrote 'There has never been a cricket book quite like this . . . David Foot has written it with compassion, something not far from passion, and sympathy. It is a remarkable achievement . . .'

Gimblett himself was something of a Somerset mystery. The epitome of Somerset cricket, a buccaneer of a batsman, he scored more than 23,000 runs in first-class cricket and yet played in a mere three test matches for

Harold Gimblett

46

Alfoxton Park, the home of Wordsworth and his sister Dorothy.

England. A complex man, Gimblett took his own life in 1978. Maybe this lack of selection for England lay behind the man's brooding, often depressed personality. Or perhaps Somerset was in those days, 'an unfashionable county'. Harold Stephenson, for example, was a hugely successful wicket-keeper. His pads may have looked too big for him, but he was responsible for a thousand dismissals – yet not a single England cap. Bill Andrews too suffered the same fate: Bill with a classic bowling action, the best handwriting and the biggest barrel of cricketing stories, took 768 wickets for his county. Less talented men have taken the new ball for England.

We seem to have strayed from creativity, but then that's Somerset.

For one of the great chapters of Somerset creativity we have to go back to the 1700s: to the north coast. The coastline lies beneath the glorious Quantocks. This was the wandering territory of Coleridge and Wordsworth. Wordsworth and his sister Dorothy lived at Alfoxton Park: a Queen Anne house perfectly set in a hollow on the slopes of the hills. Surrounded on three sides by fifty acres of woods and parkland, the fourth side has views across the Bristol Channel to the coast of Wales. The house was leased to the poet, who came on the suggestion of Samuel Taylor Coleridge, then living at nearby Nether Stowey.

A sparkling social circle of writers and free thinking intellectuals visited Alfoxton at this time. They included writers Charles Lamb, Thomas de Quincey and Robert Southey; the political theorists William Hazlitt and John Thelwall; the scientist Sir Humphry Davy; and the industrialist and philanthropist Josiah Wedgwood, and his brothers.

Today Alfoxton Park is a country house hotel, and an ancient oak, mentioned by Dorothy Wordsworth in her journal, still stands in the grounds.

Coleridge lived in a very different residence. Today a National Trust property, it was then a lonely farmhouse – and here he wrote his most enduring works.

One day, out walking with Dorothy in the direction of Watchett, Coleridge began to compose *The Rime of the Ancient Mariner*. The three resolved to shape a poem which would earn them £5 – enough to pay for their lunch and tea on the day's outing!

Watchet is the port from which the unfortunate sailor set out to dangerous seas:

> 'The ship was cheered,
> the harbour cleared,
> merrily did we drop,
> Below the kirk, below the hill,
> Below the lighthouse top.'

Certainly there is a church, St. Decuman's, ample hills too, but there is no lighthouse at Watchet. Of course, Coleridge may have been thinking of the light on Flat Holm Island in the Channel.

In the end, the poem made Coleridge rather more than the price of lunch and tea and Wordsworth who contributed only two lines, sportingly declined any rights.

It was at Nether Stowey that Coleridge 'wrote' Kubla Khan, whose curious origin he described himself in the third person:

'In consequence of a slight indisposition, an anodyne had been prescribed from the effects of which he fell asleep in his chair at the moment that he was reading the following sentence, or words of the same substance, in Purchas's *Pilgrimage*: "Here the Khan Kubla commanded a palace to be built, and a stately garden thereunto. And thus ten miles of fertile ground were enclosed by a wall." The author continued for about three hours in a profound sleep, at least of the external senses, during which time he has the most vivid confidence that he could not have composed less than from two to three hundred lines; if that indeed can be called composition in which all the images rose up before him as things, with a parallel production of the corresponding expressions, without any sensation or consciousness of effect. On awaking he appeared to himself to have a distinct recollection of the whole, and, taking his pen, ink and paper, instantly and eagerly wrote down the lines that are preserved. At this moment he was unfortunately called out by a person on business from Porlock, and detained by him above an hour, and on his return to his room found, to his no small surprise and mortification, that though he still retained some vague and dim recollection of the general purport of the vision, yet, with the exception of some eight or ten scattered lines and images, all the rest had passed away like the images on the surface of a stream into which a stone has been cast, but, alas! without the after restoration of the latter.'

We do not know for certain whether Coleridge had in 1797 begun to use opium – soon to dominate his life and rob him of his gifts. Nor do we know the identity of the 'person' from Porlock or the nature of his business.

Was he from the Secret Service? Rumour and talk had given rise to local suspicion that Coleridge, the Wordsworths and some of their radical visitors were somehow connected with spying for Bonaparte?

All is now shrouded in mystery – we shall never know the answers.

Some say creative insights rise to consciousness very much as though they come from some other sources. Thackeray in *Roundabout Papers* said: 'I have been surprised at the observations made by some of my characters. It seems as if an occult power was moving the pen,' and Keats said that he had 'not been aware of the beauty of some thought or expression' until *after* he had written it down on paper – on reflection Keats felt such words had been written 'by someone else.'

Maybe that kind of chemistry is especially strong here in Somerset.

And now . . .

AS BEFITS an experienced broadcaster and skilful interviewer, Polly Lloyd has a natural curiosity. Her first television interview was at a nudist club. Typical of Scorpio, she has something of Miss Marple in her make-up.

Polly and I share a curious coincidence – with strong Supernatural undertones. Back in 1987 we at Bossiney were planning an expansion into Dorset, and I was looking for a new author to do a book Legends of Dorset. Though Polly and I had not met, I had heard her broadcasting on B.B.C. Radio Bristol on a number of occasions. She struck me as the kind of person who might be interested in writing a book, and backing that simple hunch I phoned her one afternoon.

'I'd love to . . .' said an astonished Polly. 'But I can hardly believe this conversation is taking place . . .' She went on to explain that on that very morning she had consulted a clairvoyant who had told her: 'Your career is going to take on a new dimension in that you're going to become an author!'

Anyway she did such a superb job with Legends of Dorset that we asked her to contribute a chapter to Wiltshire Mysteries and, more recently, she contributed About Exmoor to the Bossiney list. This is Polly's third Bossiney title in four years – clearly a remarkable coincidence or proof of second sight – or maybe both.

Polly Lloyd is a considerable all-rounder: a gifted communicator through radio and television and a thoughtful, perceptive writer. She may write about legends but she has the wit and wisdom to know that there is no such thing as pure myth, and equally she understands that real people can – and do – become living legends. Talking and travelling with her is invariably a worthwhile experience, and such is the quality of her writing that we, the reader, can somehow travel by proxy.

Her harvesting can be of contrast: she can research deeply or, like the genesis of a Daphne du Maurier story, it can be something observed, something overheard, a whole theme triggered. In the media she has interviewed all types and temperaments: politicians and poets, cricketers and crackpots, actresses and aldermen, vicars and victims. Consequently she can sense – almost scent – the phoney, but she probes with good manners, and, like Sue Lawley or Anna Ford, she retains a sense of objectivity – and it is this quality which makes her such a valued colleague in the Supernatural field. Whether she is investigating the Glastonbury Zodiac or visiting a haunted property, she remains a true professional.

For the remainder of this journey through mysterious Somerset, you travel with Polly. You could not have a better, more uderstanding companion.

Polly Lloyd at work in the broadcasting studio.

Introducing Polly Lloyd

*P*OLLY LLOYD *was born in Liverpool, but has lived in Bristol since she was a teenager. She is married with a son and daughter, and various pets.*

A Scorpio subject, she joined B.B.C. Radio Bristol in 1980 as a secretary. 'Then one day, I was asked to read a listener's letter on air, and instinctively knew: "This is what I want to do!" ' Polly has had a variety of roles in radio, most recently four years presenting a daily programme. Now she combines radio with T.V. work as well as writing.

She lists the theatre, books and gardening as her principal interests and for some years was a member of an amateur dance group which raised money for charity. In 1987 she visited Egypt and produced and presented a B.B.C. Radio Bristol cassette on Ancient Egypt and Egypt today.

She enjoys the research for her books, visiting the sites, working in libraries, and checking out museums. This is Polly's fourth contribution to the Bossiney list.

Polly relaxing at the Doone Valley Riding Stables, Malmsmead, on Exmoor.

Burrow Mump, 75 feet high and crowned with a ruined chapel dedicated to St. Michael. It is now a memorial to the men of Somerset who died during the last war.

THE SHAPING OF SOMERSET

IN HIS definition of the word 'mystery' at the beginning of this book my co-author quotes 'a person or thing that arouses curiosity or suspense because of an unknown, obscure or enigmatic quality'. How apt that definition is when applied to aspects of the county's history. Historians are always curious to learn about the mystery of times gone by, to uncover the unknown, to make clear the obscure, to explain the enigmatic. It helps us not only build up a picture of life throughout the ages but also understand the influence our ancestors have had on the way we live today. Sometimes we are surprised to discover how sophisticated they were, sometimes it is their primitive behaviour that intrigues us. Looking back to the earliest history of the county, there are many episodes which tell us a good deal about the shaping of Somerset, but still retain an element of mystery.

The Romans, for example, left their mark on Somerset. The Roman Empire was vast, of course, and Somerset lay on the outermost limits, far, far from Rome. Consequently the arrival of the Romans in the West country was heralded not so much by a violent invasion as by an infiltration of Roman sophistication and culture. The city of Bath epitomises the Roman way of life in Britain with its spa water and the Roman Baths which are visited by tourists from all over the world. The Romans called it Aquae Sulis, and the treasures they left behind are so famous they really do not need to be recounted here. But other Roman settlements are worth a mention because they influenced Somerset life in those early centuries.

Two important centres were Ilchester and Charterhouse-on-Mendip. Ilchester – or Lindinis – was a typical Roman market centre serving the surrounding farming communities such as that found at Bradley Hill near Somerton. Excavations show that the farm revolved around what was in essence an extended family, an orderly structured way of life so beloved of the Romans. Charterhouse, on the other hand, was a lead mining centre, the lead being used to supply areas much further afield. Its importance is

A family of ducks swim serenely along a rhine on the Somerset Levels ...

demonstrated by the fact that the only amphitheatre in Somerset was at Charterhouse.

Wherever the Romans went, they built straight sweeping roads, a symbol of their unwavering confidence and intellectual superiority, an arrogance in a way. They did it in Somerset too – the famous Fosse Way cuts across from north east to south west, for example – and on the whole they settled close by their highways. But other Roman ruins have been found scattered throughout the county, each one telling us a little bit more about the shaping of Somerset.

The foundations of one such villa lie almost forgotten beneath the grass in a field close to the coast in the north of old Somerset, at Wemberham near Yatton. We tend to think of the Somerset Levels as being that central part of Somerset around Glastonbury but there is a stretch of land that skirts the western edge of the Mendips and follows the coast roughly from Brean Down to Clevedon. Here too the land is low-lying, prone to flooding, drained by a system of ditches and rhines which take the water off the land

Ken Stuckey

in the wet winter months, and bring fresh water down from the lakes and reservoirs to irrigate it during the dry summer months. A sea wall further protects the land, and the salt water is kept at bay by a series of sluice gates. Occasionally, the system fails in the face of exceptional tides and storms.

There is a plaque in the church at Kingston Seymour which tells of:

January 20th 1606 and 4th of Jas I.

An innundation of sea water by overflowing and breaking down the sea banks happened in this parish of Kingstone Seamore and many others adjoining; by reason whereof many persons were drowned and much cattle and goods were lost: the water in the Church was five feet high and the greatest part lay on the ground about ten days.

On the whole the system has served the area well for centuries. But just how many centuries man has – more or less – held the upper hand in this part of old Somerset is a mystery. The forgotten Roman villa at Wemberham provides a vital clue as I learned from a man called Ken Stuckey.

Ken Stuckey farmed at Kingston Seymour, not far from Wemberham, for many years. He is a natural observer whose love of the countryside and knowledge of tradition, coupled with an inquiring mind, make him an ideal guide to the history of the locality. I have spent many happy hours talking to Ken, and sharing his stories with my radio listeners, and one day we drove together down the lanes and across the fields to the site of the villa.

The landscape here is flat and open. The Romans had an eye for a perfect setting, and here on the banks of the River Yeo they built their villa. Ken told me it must have been a sizeable construction with about ten rooms including a kitchen, a women's apartment, a servants' hall and a store room. There were two courtyards, one large and one small, and some beautiful tesselated floors. The Romans liked their creature comforts, so the whole thing was heated by an effective hypocaust system. There was a library and a chapel, and listening to Ken describing it, it was easy to picture a small, civilised community going about their daily tasks and duties in that gentle, pastoral setting.

There seems also to have been access to the river itself, although a certain amount of mystery surrounds this aspect of the building. Two walls, three feet thick, run from the villa into the river bank – and disappear. There is no sign of them on the other side of the bank. It seems probable though that this is how cargoes were moved from boat to villa in some way. The river would have been quite busy bringing goods down from places further inland, or up from the sea. The land around the villa was more than likely to have been well cultivated, suggesting a two-way trade. Great Wemberham Field close by is mentioned in the Doomsday Book, the most important field locally, and was probably cultivated in Roman times.

The villa was discovered in 1884 on land owned by the Smyth-Pigotts, a leading family in that area. Mr Smyth-Pigott was a keen archaeologist and had the whole excavation covered with a galvanised roof while work was carried out. Many visitors came to watch the progress. The Somerset Archaeological Society organised a trip, travelling by train to Yatton and then continuing in horse brakes. There were finds of coins and pottery, and coins from the reign of Edward III indicating a previous excavation. A hoard of eight hundred Roman coins was also found in Kingston Seymour.

Ken Stuckey remembers an elderly man who used to help on the farm when Ken was a boy. This chap used to tell stories of his time as a watchman at the site of the excavation. He used to sell off small bits of Roman clay for half a crown apiece to visitors to the villa.

Although we know so much about the villa at Wemberham, what happened next is less well documented. How much of the Roman ruins were taken away for private collections, or how much was simply covered up again, and when, we simply do not know. We don't even know for sure who owns the land today. Apparently when the Smyth-Pigotts sold the field, they sold the half acre or so which contains the villa separately. The chances of the villa being excavated again are slim.

These days the villa is forgotten by all but those with an interest in archaeology. The only hint of its existence is the merest shadow in the grass outlining the foundations. When I visited it with Ken, the sheep continued to graze around us, unperturbed by our arrival. The Yeo wound its way gently through the fields and the wind blew in from the sea. Ken smiled wryly and remarked that it needed a bit of imagination to picture it as it would have been when the Romans lived here. But to be honest, it was not too difficult to conjure up an image of life eighteen centuries ago.

But the true significance of the villa lies in its siting. Left to nature the land round here, as I have explained, would flood regularly, making it impossible to build anything successfully. In order to build the villa, the Romans must have used their engineering brilliance to control the Yeo and to drain the land. The Wemberham villa is a vital clue to the overall history of Somerset, because it answers the question about land management. It proves that it was the Romans who laid down a pattern which continues to this day. Another piece of the jigsaw slots into place.

The Romans brought with them culture, discipline, order, their advanced engineering skills, and a structured society. But long before they arrived Somerset was home to some of Britain's earliest inhabitants. During the Old Stone Age, a pre-historic period that covered many thousands of years, the climate changed several times. In warmer periods, men ventured out to camp near water, but in the interim cold periods they took shelter in caves, living in small groups, hunting and gathering plant food. Somerset was one part of Britain where these people lived.

Somerset's caves are justifiably famous. They provide a real challenge to the serious caver and you can read various accounts of underground expeditions. Parts of the network of caves are still uncharted. The more accessible caves, at Cheddar and at Wookey, attract thousands of visitors each year, tourists who come to marvel at the magnificence of the caves themselves, to thrill to the legends, to enjoy the attractions which have been provided by enterprising businessmen. It is a great way to spend a day, and quite awesome to realise that these spectacular caves were once home to our ancestors.

It is difficult to come to terms with just how far back in history these communities flourished. The birth of Christ two thousand years ago has some sort of perspective for us, but to think of people living in Somerset thirty five thousand years before that is not so easy to grasp. But the evidence is there to prove it, throughout the Mendip Caves. For example, Hyena Den at Wookey is believed to have been occupied from 35,000 B.C. until about 12,000 B.C. During the final cold phases of the Ice Age wild animals, main-

Cheddar Gorge, one of the wonders of Somerset.

ly the eponymous hyena, shared this large chamber with the hunters of the time. The animals left behind them huge quantities of gnawed bones of other wild animals. In 1863 archaeologists began to recover these remains.

The hunters probably had to fight off the hyenas and the other wild creatures for supremacy in the cave – it must have been a wary co-existence – and they left behind the remains of their fires, food bones, and tools that they had made from bone and flint.

It is thought that Upper Palaeolithic people lived in Soldiers Hole at Cheddar between 30,000 B.C. and 28,000 B.C., judging from some flint blades found there. And finds at Flint Jack's Cave indicate that it was inhabited briefly around 12,000 B.C. Gough's Cave, arguably Cheddar Gorge's most famous cave, has revealed many clues to Somerset's past. It seems to have been occupied during Romano-British times, that is to say relatively late for cave dwelling, and also much earlier during the Iron Age. Flint implements and tools have been found in the lower levels of the cave, together with ornaments fashioned from bone and shell. It would seem that quite large numbers of people lived here between 12,000 and 8,000 B.C.

Piecing together the available information we begin to build up a picture of life within the caves. We can imagine families grouped around their fire, the flames throwing shadows onto the cave walls, men and women cooking meat to eat, making tools for hunting and butchering, for cutting skins to wear. Primitive people, yes, but sufficiently civilised to want to add simple ornaments to their clothing, pins made from bone and shell. Wild animals may have lurked in the dark recesses of the cave, or prowled around the wild countryside howling into the wind. With a little imagination, we can paint a vivid picture, and develop an understanding of prehistoric man.

But mystery remains. Among the finds at both Cheddar and at Wookey Hole there is evidence of the slaughter of human beings. The question is, why did these people die?

The finds at Gough's Cave include something that could be a ceremonial staff. It is quite obviously incomplete and has been made from a reindeer antler. It has been carefully drilled at one end and the shaft has been decorated. It was found buried alongside an adult man. French archaeologists called it a 'bâton de commandement'. Another complete example, this time made of human bone, was also found in the cave. The significance of these staffs has yet to be established. Who was the man buried with the reindeer antler? Was he an important member of the community buried with due ceremony, the staff a symbol of his high standing? Or was he perhaps a human sacrifice? The latter explanation would suggest that these primitive people held some sort of pagan belief which involved a degree of ritual.

Human bones have also been uncovered at Wookey Hole, and here the sinister interpretation of the finds is cannibalism. Animal bones found in

An old photograph of Tarr Steps near Dulverton

the cave had been broken open for the marrow – and so seemingly had human bones. Remember, these were people who had reached a certain level of civilisation, who had risen above the basic fight for survival. To think of them turning to cannibalism may seem shocking. But conditions during the Old Stone Age could be extremely severe, and faced with starvation, cannibalism may have been the only alternative.

It is important when we imagine life in the caves not to paint too cosy a picture. It is important, too, not to judge too harshly by twentieth century ideals. The technology of archaeology improves all the time, uncovering more detailed evidence, and offering more accurate explanation to confirm – or deny – more theories. Perhaps one day we will have a definitive description of pre-historic life. Until then, the Mendip Caves and the people who inhabited them will remain a Somerset mystery.

There is another episode in the shaping of Somerset which is perhaps the most fascinating of all. It is hidden in the peat fields near Glastonbury and represents some of man's earliest efforts to overcome the problems set by a difficult landscape. Thousands of years ago, faced with land which was at certain times too wet to walk across, but not sufficiently flooded to travel by boat, the early inhabitants of Somerset built themselves trackways across the levels, simple but effective constructions that enabled them to travel from A to B in safety and comfort.

Once again, I was lucky enough to visit the area in the company of an articulate and knowledgeable guide – Bryony Coles. Bryony and her husband Dr John Coles spent a number of years working in the vicinity, excavating and analysing, and in the mid-1980s published their excellent account, *Sweet Track to Glastonbury, (pub. Thames and Hudson)*. Their work is of the very highest academic standard, but putting the whole thing in layman's terms for my benefit, Bryony painted a sparkling picture of life six thousand years ago.

The Somerset Levels, because they are so low-lying, have always been prone to flooding. These days they are controlled by a series of ditches and rhines, but thousands of years ago it was possible to travel from 'island' to 'island' by boat, so deeply were they flooded. In between times, when the floods receded, the land was too wet and heavy underfoot to be safe to walk across, and so prehistoric man set about building wooden tracks across the marshes. As the centuries passed these tracks became buried beneath layers of peat, whose natural properties preserved them more or less intact. Peat cutting eventually uncovered the treasures; the increased demand for peat for horticultural purposes in the 1960s, 1970s and 1980s has accelerated the rate of cutting.

Wooden trackway across the Levels ... ▶

The first track was discovered towards the end of the nineteenth century and the renowned archaeologist Dr Arthur Bulleid investigated it. It stretched from Meare to Edington Burtle and because it lay several feet below the surface of the earth was at first thought to be a secret tunnel. Because there were monastic buildings at Westhay and a priory at Edington, it was named the Abbot's Way but of course we know now that it was a surface pathway, and furthermore, it was built about 2,500 B.C., long before there were any abbots!

The people who built the tracks were among the earliest farmers in the British Isles. They lived on an area of raised bog in the middle of marshes, surrounded by moss, sedges and cotton grass, which decomposed in time to form peat. The tracks were made of planks split from alder, with slats and branches filling the gaps. The peat has perfectly preserved the tracks, but is now being cut at quite a rate. The peat companies however have worked in conjunction with the archaeologists, calling them in to investigate finds, and preserving important pieces of land from cutting. Dr John Coles first began work here in the 1960s; the Somerset Levels Project was set up in the 1970s and brought Bryony Coles to the area. The work has been painstaking and detailed, using the latest scientific methods to gather as much information as possible, and to date the finds accurately.

There are a number of trackways in the vicinity. Some, for example the Walton Heath Track, and the Eclipse Track, were covered with woven hurdles, the earliest examples of a craft which continues today. You can see a perfectly preserved hurdle from the Walton Heath Track in the County Museum in Taunton.

The most significant track however was discovered relatively recently. It was found in 1970 by sharp-eyed peat cutter Mr Ray Sweet, and named in his honour. And what an honour, because this find turned out to be a trackway built around 4,000 B.C., the earliest trackway on the Levels and believed to be the oldest road not only in Britain but in the whole of Europe.

Unlike the Abbot's Way, which had to contend with hummocks and pools and curved accordingly, the Sweet Track is very straight. It is about 1,800 metres long, the planks made of oak and ash, the pegs of hazel, alderwood, ash and holly. The trees would have been cut with stone axes and wooden mallets from raised land nearby, and then carried to the marsh, hard physical labour. The actual laying of the track however was quite straightforward. John and Bryony Coles tried to build a stretch of track themselves and found the construction so simple and efficient that probably the whole track could have been laid in a day or two. When the tracks are exposed to the elements, the timber dries out at an alarming rate, and would soon be destroyed, so the Sweet Track has been covered up again to preserve it, and the earth is kept suitably damp by pumping water on to it whenever necessary. The land in which it lies now belongs to the Nature Conservancy Council; when the track was laid it would have cut through tall reeds and sedge, today yellow irises and royal fern flourish all around.

Although the Sweet Track was built so long ago, thanks to the work of John and Bryony Coles and the Somerset Levels Project we are able to build up a graphic picture of what it must have looked like and a great deal of information has been collected. Modern techniques are so sophisticated that, for example, we know that all the timber used to build the Sweet Track was cut during the course of one winter. But the people who built the tracks and used them to cross the Levels remain much more of a mystery.

We know they were amongst the first farmers in Britain, keeping cattle and sheep and cultivating cereals. We know they hunted birds and deer because of the arrow heads that have been found. We know they had plenty of wild fruit, blackberries, elderberries, sloes and apples. We are not sure exactly what their homes looked like but we can make an educated guess. We know they were good at cutting oak planks, and we know from pollen tests that there was an ample supply of reeds which could have been used for thatching, so in all probability their homes were warm and waterproof. We know they made pottery but we are not certain what they wore.

They may have made their clothes from leather and also from a fabric woven from plant fibre – nettle fibre rather than linen. We can assume a certain amount but more than that remains a mystery, because the peat, perfect for preserving wood, is too acid to preserve skeletons. Of man, beast and bird nothing remains. Only a few beetles have been found.

Some tantalising treasures have been uncovered on the Levels dating back to the times when the tracks were being used. A small parcel of flint flakes, unused and carefully wrapped in layers of moss and cotton grass dates from around 2,200 B.C. A maple wood box containing bronze tools and ornaments was found near Edington Burtle. It must have belonged to a farmer, or possibly a merchant, who may have buried it for safe keeping around 1,500 B.C. An amber necklace – a real treasure – was found near Godney Moor. The amber came originally from Jutland.

How fascinating all this is, to know so much about life so long ago, to have the means of extracting important information from the finds, to share the knowledge of dedicated archaeologists like the Coles, and indeed their predecessors such as Arthur Bulleid. Some of the discoveries are on display at museums, the County Museum in Taunton, the Tribunal at Glastonbury and the Woodspring Museum at Weston-super-Mare, and there is a very good exhibition in the heart of the Levels at the Peat Moors Visitor Centre at Westhay.

But what the story of the trackways has in common with the Mendip

Cave dwellers, and the Romans who made their home in Somerset is that element of mystery. There is a point where our knowledge ends and we can only use our imagination – albeit a well-informed imagination – to fill in the gaps. It is possible that in time we will have the means to uncover the last remaining secrets; after all, fifty years ago who would have believed we would be able to carbon-date items so accurately. But until then we have to content ourselves with a little intrigue, and allow Somerset to retain some of its mysteries.

THE GLASTONBURY ZODIAC

IN ANY account of the mysteries of Somerset, Glastonbury must be the jewel in the crown. Its distinctive Tor draws visitors from far and wide, and its legends of Joseph of Arimathea and King Arthur and his knights are famous. Less well documented is the discovery earlier this century of a pattern of symbols and shapes which lie hidden in the landscape. Outlined by brooks, streams and ditches, by hedges, paths and lanes, detailed by hillocks and woods, they are invisible to the untutored eye. But once revealed, it becomes apparent that they form a complete zodiac, ancient beyond memory.

The secrets of the Glastonbury Zodiac were lost with the passage of time, and the figures lay hidden and forgotten until a remarkable woman called Katharine Maltwood stumbled across the key which was to unlock for her the whole marvellous mystery.

Born in 1878 in Woodland Green in Essex, photographs of Katharine show a clear-eyed, dark-haired girl with a calm strong face. In photographs taken later in her life, the eyes are still a striking feature. She studied sculpture at the Slade, and exhibited at the Royal Academy, her work often based on a mystical theme. She married her childhood sweetheart, John Maltwood, who adored her. 'She was a goddess' he told a disciple of Katharine's work after his wife's death. Although quite poor at the time of their marriage, John Maltwood became a wealthy man and was able to provide a comfortable life for Katharine which left her free to develop her artistic skills, and to study the mythical subjects her inquiring mind found so fascinating.

In the late 1920s she grew interested in the Arthurian legend, and was invited by the publishers of *The High History of the Holy Grail*, a book which had just been translated from a Norman-French manuscript, to draw an itinerary of the quest for the Grail in Avalon. The manuscript was a strange

Overleaf:The Battle of Sedgemoor, a bloody milestone in Somerset's history ▶

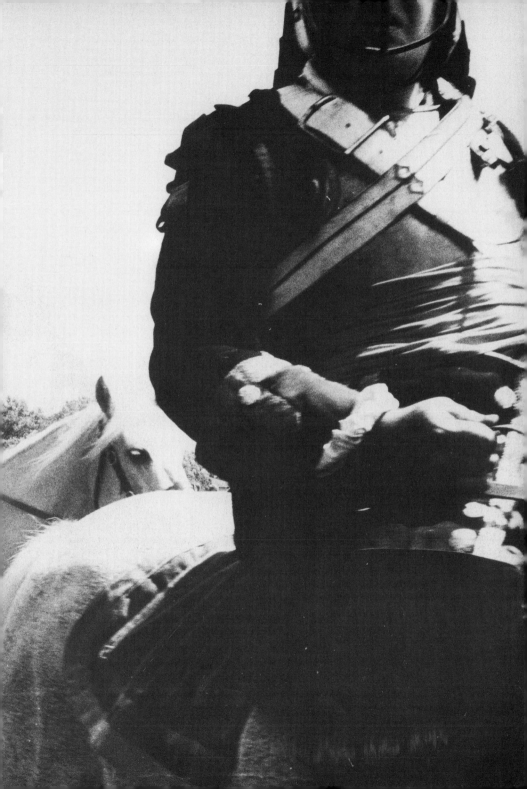

mystical text, reputedly written many centuries ago at Glastonbury Abbey. It was full of allegory and symbolism, but Katharine's studies soon showed that the adventures of the knights matched exactly places in the Vale of Avalon. And it was while following in their footsteps, tracing their encounters with lions, dragons and giants, that she discovered, mapped out in the landscape, a huge lion, its belly drawn by the River Cary, its back outlined by Somerton Lane, an ancient road. Her next discovery was of a giant man, marked out quite clearly to her. It was a discussion with an astrologer friend that led her to believe these two figures might represent Leo and Gemini, signs of the zodiac, and armed with this clue, she set about uncovering the entire Zodiac which had lain in oblivion for so long.

Katharine Maltwood published her theory in 1935 in a book called *Glastonbury's Temple of the Stars*. It is an astonishing revelation. The twelve signs of the zodiac, precisely and accurately placed within a circle roughly ten miles in diameter, are traced by boundaries both natural and manmade. The horns of Taurus the bull stretch out from Hatch Hill, the Scorpion's tail stings the rump of Sagittarius's horse at Withial, the back of Capricorn the Goat is marked by the road from Glastonbury to Shepton Mallett.

Furthermore, Katharine and later her followers, showed that layer upon layer of legend links the Glastonbury Zodiac with other great sagas told by Celtic bards and Norse story tellers, with the visiting Romans, and with the search for the Holy Grail and of course with Arthur and his knights. The name of villages, farms and inns, of lanes and hills and woods reflect time and time again the ancient images which seem obscure to modern minds but which once would have been more readily apparent. Katharine believed the Glastonbury Zodiac was formed by nature, and that men were guided by an unseen hand to construct their roads and ditches, to plant their fields and hedges in a way which enhanced and reaffirmed the outlines. Expanding on her original studies, developing her thoughts, Katharine and her followers discovered a mystic pattern which is both reassuring in its harmony and awesome in its complexity.

And yet, there must be doubts. Although the signs are accurately placed in accordance with the stars that mirror them, their outlines are less than perfect. Indeed three are completely different from orthodox signs, Aquarius being depicted as a phoenix, Libra as a dove and Cancer as a boat. Can it really be possible that the features of the Somerset landscape, both those formed by nature and those made by man, should have changed so little throughout all those centuries that the signs remain intact? Is there not a suspicious readiness to tie up loose ends, a somewhat cavalier linking of coincidences? And does it not take a generous and accepting eye to discernthe shapes at all?

The Theatre Royal, Bath, historic and beautiful, as is so much of Somerset. ▶

Katharine believed *The High History of the Holy Grail* was written by a Templar, and the historian Geoffrey Ashe, who has studied her findings, believes that the Glastonbury Zodiac was known to Nostradamus who referred to it as the 'great heavenly temple:'

'In the land of the great heavenly temple
A nephew at London is murdered through a false peace',
the nephew being the Duke of Monmouth whose army was defeated at nearby Sedgemoor and who was subsequently beheaded by his uncle James II. But both these claims are based on interpretations of enigmatic texts, and interpretation is always open to challenge. All in all, it is very easy for academics and scientists, pointing to a noticeable lack of hard evidence, to dismiss the whole business as the over-enthusiastic conclusions of eager students. People, say the cynics, see what they want to see. In a rational world, there is no room for the Glastonbury Zodiac.

But in a rational world there is no room for mystery. Geoffrey Ashe describes Katharine's understanding of the Zodiac as 'psychological and spiritual' rather than 'archaeological' and those who are intrigued to know what lies behind myth and legend will appreciate the sentiment. Some people see pictures in a fire where others see only flames, some see dark landscapes where others see only clouds. Perhaps it is just half the story to say that people see what they want to see. Perhaps people see what they can see – and some are more perceptive than others.

SEDGEMOOR

CHEDZOY, Middlezoy, Westonzoyland – names with a true Somerset ring to them, and home to a part of Somerset's history that is inextricably interwoven with the history of England itself. For this is Sedgemoor, broad acres of flat, fertile land, prone to flooding and drained by a criss-cross of rhynes or man-made ditches. Sedgemoor – scene of the last battle fought on English soil.

On Sunday July 5th 1685, the Duke of Monmouth, illegitimate son of Charles II, climbed the tower of St Mary's Parish Church in Bridgwater and looked out over Sedgemoor. On the death of his father the crown had passed not to him, but to his uncle James II, a papist. Monmouth had landed at Lyme on June 11th, returning from exile with about eighty followers, determined to claim the crown for himself and to make England once more a Protestant country.

He had gathered support along the way – about six thousand rebels in all – and at Taunton he had been proclaimed rightful monarch, but now he faced his sternest test. About one quarter of the British Standing Army, led by the Earl of Feversham, was advancing on the uprising and a battle was inevitable.

Monmouth realised that a daylight attack was out of the question. His troops were outnumbered, untrained and armed only with home-made weapons. But a night attack might just succeed, and as Monmouth and his advisers climbed down from their vantage point, their plans were laid. In the early hours of July 6th, under cover of darkness, Monmouth's men moved quietly forward.

At first all seemed to be going well, but suddenly a shot rang out – some say it was fired by a traitor – and alerted the King's army, which was camped behind the great Bussex Rhyne. From that moment it was a lost cause. The

Author Polly Lloyd reading the memorial to all those who fell at the Battle of Sedgemoor on July 6 1685.

rebel cavalry could not cover the whole Royal Front. Their ranks were broken into small groups by the volleys fired at them from across the rhine. Their horses, untrained to gunshot, panicked, spreading alarm and disorder as they bolted through the foot soldiers.

Monmouth fled, together with Lord Grey, leaving his men to fight a hopeless and bloody battle. The Pitchfork Rebellion, fishermen, weavers, miners and farm labourers from Dorset, Devon and Somerset, faced the trained and disciplined troops of the Royal Army. Hundreds died, many more were horribly wounded, the rest faced rough justice under a charge of treason. Monmouth himself was captured and was shortly afterwards beheaded on his uncle's orders at the Tower of London.

Such violence and bloodshed left a deep imprint on the Somerset countryside, and not surprisingly, there are many stories of ghosts around Sedgemoor. There are claims that the ghost of a man, headless and on foot, is that of Monmouth himself, haunting a house at Catcott where he is reputed to have stayed before the battle. Others believe that Monmouth returns on horseback, wearing the high boots and broad brimmed hat of the times, his cloak flying out behind him as he gallops silently eastwards, away from Sedgemoor. Similar figures have been seen many times, spirits perhaps of other rebels, local men who fought for their Protestant faith. Peter Underwood, President of the Ghost Club, notes that the ghost of Monmouth is said to appear each year on July 3rd – notwithstanding the fact that the battle took place on the 6th.

At the Bussex Rhyne, where so many men from both sides died in a brief but bloody battle, phantom soldiers, weary and ragged have been seen, and on one occasion at least, a band of them appeared, armed with pikes and staves. People say that voices can be heard from time to time, as well as the distant sound of fierce hand-to-hand combat, and – chillingly – calls to 'Come over and fight'.

There is a sad story of a young girl whose ghost is said to haunt the area. Her sweetheart, captured by the King's army, was admired as a swift runner, and hearing this, his captors promised him his freedom if he could keep pace with a galloping horse. Valiantly, fear and desperation giving him speed, he ran neck and neck with the beast, only to be executed anyway. His distraught lady drowned herself. And another heartbreaking tale concerns a woman at Locking, wife of the Lord of the Manor, Sir John Plumley. Their two sons fell at Sedgemoor, and Sir John himself fled and hid from the King's army when he realised the battle was lost. Unfortunately, his over-zealous guard dog gave the game away and he was discovered, taken

The parish church of St. Mary's Bridgwater. The Duke of Monmouth climbed the tower to look across Sedgemoor on the eve of the battle.

The last battle on English soil, commemorated in this inn sign.

away and hanged. His wife took the dog and plunged with it in her arms into the Manor well. Her ghost and that of the dog are seen together between two yew trees before disappearing into the now disused well.

There are many ghostly stories connected with the area around Sedgemoor, well-documented accounts of galloping horses as well as those of soldiers. And there are stories connected with events after the battle, when the rebel 'traitors' were dealt with. Many were summarily hung from the great oak at Heddon, and reports from there of the sounds of clanking chains and frightened moans, together with horses' hooves, are numerous. Certain crossroads, the sites of gibbets, share that reputation.

Later the Hanging Judge, Judge Jeffreys, arrived to dispense his own particular brand of justice. An ambitious and hard hearted man, he sent scores of people to their deaths and ordered countless more to be transported to the colonies, as his court circulated throughout the Westcountry, and his restless spirit seems to haunt a number of different places. One such is the Tudor Tavern where he stayed while he was holding trials in Taunton – indeed some believe he also held his court at that inn. But it seems more likely that his victims were brought before him in the Great Hall of Taunton Castle, and heavy footsteps are heard here, dragging reluctant prisoners to face the Judge.

Ironically, Monmouth too stayed at Taunton Castle (now an hotel) before moving on towards Sedgemoor, and memories of those last hopeful days linger. The ghostly music of a long-dead violinist has been heard, a violinist who helped the duke and his men 'eat, drink and be merry' as they prepared for battle, brave men unaware that they were spending their last few days on this earth.

To those who believe that actions and events are imprinted on town and country, that happenings and emotions are recorded as it were by their surroundings to be replayed in the form of ghostly visitations, it is not surprising that an event as powerful and important as the Battle of Sedgemoor should have so many echoes. Some people hoped that perhaps the Duke of Monmouth would return to Sedgemoor on the three hundredth anniversary of the Battle, when the Sealed Knot staged a magnificent re-enactment, but his spirit stayed away.

One final thought before we leave the story of Sedgemoor, where the Bussex Rhyne led to Monmouth's downfall. Legend has it that some years earlier a gypsy warned the Duke 'beware of the rhine.' Who knows what different stories would be told today, what different ghosts would haunt the fields and lanes of Sedgemoor, what different course history would have followed if he had taken heed of her warning.

Taunton Castle, where the defeated rebels were tried by Judge Jeffreys

ALFRED THE GREAT

T HE LEGENDS of King Arthur and the Knights of the Round Table and their association with Somerset are well established and well documented – indeed an entire industry has grown up around them. But Somerset can boast connections with another king, a king who played a vital role in the course of English history, a king whose courage and leadership earned him the title 'the Great'.

He was Alfred the Great, known to generations of schoolchildren as the king who let the cakes burn and was berated by an angry peasant woman for doing so. In truth he was an intelligent and capable man who inspired great loyalty. By the age of seven he had twice visited Rome, once with his father, and in adulthood would send gifts to the Pope, a symbol of his status, his equal standing with the Holy Father. His travels doubtless gave him a wider perspective, a broader view of life than most Anglo-Saxon princelings. He was an educated man, although he could not read English until he was twelve and struggled well into middle age to master Latin. From his mother he learned to listen to the people. She taught him the old songs which carried with them a wealth of tradition and legend.

Alfred had the advantage of noble lineage – he was a descendent of Ceawlin and grandson of Egbert – but as the fifth son it seemed unlikely that he would ever become king and he grew up without that burden of responsibility. But when the time came he proved himself to be able and courageous, and ready for his new duty.

Alfred became king of Wessex in 871 following the death of his brother Ethelred. It was a turbulent time. For thirty years or so, the Danes had been periodically raiding England, at first confining their attacks to the coastlines and rivers, targets that could be reached by boat. Eventually however, they began to attack further inland and by 870 had conquered Northumbria and East Anglia. They seemed to be invincible – until they set their sights on Wessex. Wessex proved to be the strongest of the Saxon kingdoms and although the Danes were not beaten outright, they were

The Isle of Athelney, where Alfred made his secret camp, and now merely a ridge of land near the village of East Lyng. The Alfred Memorial was erected in 1801 by one Colonel John Slade.

held at bay. Twice the Danish leader Guthrum made an uneasy peace with Alfred but in 878 the Danes caught him by surprise and captured Chippenham, turning it into a Danish stronghold.

Much of Wessex submitted to Guthrum, some noblemen fled abroad and by Easter, Alfred, together with some loyal followers, had retreated to Athelney in the heart of the Somerset Levels which was at that time effectively an island. Indeed Asser, who was Alfred's friend, adviser and biographer, described it as 'surrounded on all sides by vast impassable marshes and pools so that it was totally inaccessible except by boat and a single causeway.' And it was at Athelney that Alfred waited for the right moment to win back Wessex.

Alfred was in double danger at that point for, Hubba, the youngest of three famous warrior brothers, sailed up the west coast which meant Alfred and his followers could have been crushed between two Danish forces. Hubba was flying his battle standard which reputedly had magic powers. It was painted with a raven to represent the war god Odin, but when he landed, the banner failed to catch the wind and the raven's wings drooped. It was a bad omen: Hubba and his forty-strong bodyguard, together with more than eight hundred men, were slaughtered in battle by the Saxons.

Seven weeks after Easter, Alfred sent word to his fellow Saxons in Wiltshire, Dorset and Hampshire to join him at Egbert's Stone and from there they marched to Edington. How Alfred's message reached his thanes – his nobles – and how he chose the right moment to attack is a mystery. Some say he disguised himself as a minstrel and walked right into Guthrum's camp to spy on the Danes. Others say it was while his mind was occupied with battle plans that the famous cake-burning incident took place. Whatever, after a fierce battle he beat the Danes and chased Guthrum back to Chippenham, forcing him to accept defeat and furthermore to agree to embrace the Christian faith.

Three weeks later Guthrum and about thirty other Danish chiefs came to Aller near Athelney to be baptised. Guthrum took the name Athelston and

The Alfred Jewel

80

Alfred himself acted as his godfather, although this was probably more as a symbol of superiority than as an act of forgiveness. Custom decreed that the baptismal robes and the bandages which prevented the holy oil from being rubbed from the head should be removed a week later at a ceremony known as Chrism-loosening. Guthrum's Chrism-loosening took place at the palace at Wedmore, and it was there that the treaty, the Peace of Wedmore was signed. Christian Wessex was saved.

All this is an important part of English history, and a marvellous story in the telling, but there are one or two uncertain elements. No one is quite sure, for example, exactly where Hubba's boats landed, although it was probably somewhere near the Devon-Somerset border. Alfred's battle with Guthrum was fought at 'Ethandun' which is taken to be Edington. There are several Edingtons in the south-west, but historians favour the Wiltshire Edington.

And while many historians are convinced that there was a royal 'palace' at Wedmore, there are dissenting voices. Certainly Alfred owned several estates in Somerset, and Wedmore was one of them, but there is no real evidence of a palace there. Excavations carried out at Cheddar between 1952 and 1960, however, have uncovered important Saxon finds including the so-called Long Hall. This was a building some seventy-eight feet long, the walls slightly bowed to make it wider – about twenty feet across – in the middle. There were doors at each side of the centre and a third at one end. Three posts across the interior may mark a partition. The site was protected by a ditch to the north and a palisade with a gate to the east. The compound also contained some other buildings, possibly a cornmill or a fowl house.

It is believed that Alfred certainly knew this building, perhaps even built it, and it is known for a fact that the Witan, the assembly of leaders, met here in 941, 956 and 968. Some historians question whether there would have been a royal palace at Wedmore when there was obviously one so close by at Cheddar.

In 1878, the one-thousandth anniversary of the Treaty of Wedmore, archaeologists carried out extensive work at Mudgely, a hamlet just outside Wedmore where Alfred's royal home is popularly believed to have stood. They set to work in a field known locally as Court Garden, but no Saxon remains were found, although the remains of buildings many centuries old were uncovered. An account of the excavations was included in *The Wedmore Chronicle* written by the Rev Sydenham Augustine Hervey, vicar of Wedmore 1876-1898 and the son of a former Bishop of Bath and Wells. Mr Hervey was apparently something of a character, a Liberal in a Tory stronghold and a man of conviction. He took part enthusiastically in the excavations and believed that Wedmore most certainly was the place where

Astrologer Glenys Massey, who prepared the Somerset horoscope

the Chrism-loosening, and the signing of the peace treaty, took place. And in 1890 an Alfred Memorial Window – which also served to commemorate Queen Victoria's Diamond Jubilee – was unveiled at Wedmore Church.

Some eight centuries after Alfred's battle with Guthrum, in 1693, a 'jewel' was found near Athelney. It is about two inches long, shaped like a tear-drop, with a short open tube at the narrow end. It has a gold frame decorated with gold filigree and cloisonne enamel showing a male figure holding two plants. A large piece of rock crystal covers the enamel and around the edge is inscribed the Saxon phrase 'Aelfred mec heht gewyrcan' – Alfred had me made.

Known as the Alfred Jewel, its exact purpose is unclear. Obviously of great value, one can only assume that it was King Alfred, and not another Alfred, who ordered it to be made. It could be the top of a slender staff or – and this seems to me to be the most fitting suggestion – it could be an 'aestel'. What is an aestel? Again, nobody knows for sure but it is believed that an aestel was some sort of marker for a book, perhaps to help the reader follow the lines of script. Alfred was a scholarly man, and we know that he sent a copy of his own translation of Pope Gregory's *Pastoral Care* to each of his bishops. We also know that he sent with each copy an aestel worth fifty mancuses – the price of three hundred sheep or fifty oxen. In the thirteenth century a monk wrote the Latin word 'indicatorium' above the Anglo-Saxon word aestel; hence the deduction that it was a marker to help with study or public reading.

The Alfred Jewel is an exquisite piece of craftsmanship, the figure naive in the style of the period, the materials costly, the message bold and confident. The original is in the Ashmolean but there is a copy in the County Museum in Taunton. It is a beautiful puzzle that represents more than a thousand years of history and commemorates a man who fought for his kingdom and his faith against a pagan invader. It certainly qualifies as one of the most charming *and* intriguing Somerset mysteries.

Overleaf: Bystanders watch a re-enactment of the Battle of Sedgemoor – but was the battle and the fate of the rebels written in the stars?

SOMERSET
HOROSCOPES

I HAVE written earlier in this book about the Glastonbury Zodiac, and make no apologies for returning to the subject of astrology. After all, it was an astrologer who told me I would soon write my first book, and that forecast, and many others besides, proved to be so uncannily accurate that although I try to keep an open mind on all matters I find the evidence very persuasive.

The astrologer in question is a blonde-haired lady called Glenys Massey. Glenys is well known in the Bristol area, her throaty laugh and husky Geordie voice making her a popular choice for radio programmes. She first turned to astrology – as so many people do – when her life hit a particularly difficult patch. Her marriage was ending and she was faced with redundancy from her job as an art teacher. It seemed as if everything was stacked against her, and she wanted to know why. The answers that came up in the astrological reading were so perceptive they astonished her, and she decided to find out more. Glenys is the sort of person who does not do things by halves and before long she had devoured every astrology book she could lay her hands on, and taught herself how to draw up charts and interpret them.

For many years she worked solely for her own enlightenment but by 1980 she was teaching the rudiments of astrology at evening classes, and impressing her pupils with her insight. For although astrology is a science it does require a certain amount of interpretation, and quite simply some people are better at it than others. Word got round and clients began to beat a path to her door for her to look at their chart or read the tarot cards for them.

Obviously, an individual reading is much more accurate than the 'stars' in the newspapers can ever be. As Glenys explained to me, those are based on Sun Sign astrology, that is to say, the zodiac sign in which the sun was placed at the time of birth. But there are ten planets to take into consideration, as well as an Ascendant and a Midheaven, which give a more detailed picture. In other words there will be some traits in common to all those who share a particular sun sign but the rest of their affairs will differ greatly according to the placement of the remaining nine planets.

Glenys points out that regardless of whether or not people are interested in astrology, each of us automatically acquires an individual horoscope chart at birth. She says this can be loosely compared to an in-built computer programme for life which describes the potential success or failure of such things as work, health, relationships. She quotes the psychologist C.G. Jung, who wrote 'Whatever is born or done in this moment of time has the qualities of this moment of time'.

Talking to Glenys one day, she remarked that things other than people can have a birth chart or 'starting point'. For example, it is not uncommon for an astrologer to prepare a chart for the birth of a business or the date of a marriage. In some cases dates are chosen ahead of time – this is called Electional astrology. In the sixteenth century, the King of Spain used astrology to choose the date of the laying of the foundation stone of the Escorial. His empire was governed from this vast building and it was calculated that both the Sun and Moon placed in the Zodiac sign of Aries would best indicate the enterprise and warlike qualities needed for success.

Furthermore, Glenys told me, towns and cities also have starting points.

'The birth time generally accepted by astrologers,' she said, 'is the date of a charter of government, when a loose collection of settlers suddenly had a corporate identity and need of a mayor and other officials. This is known as Mundane Astrology – not because it's boring but because it comes from the Latin word for world.'

Apparently some astrologers specialise in Mundane Astrology; one such is a man called Charles E.O. Carter, who wrote in his book *Political Astrology* 'Sooner or later I believe Mundane Astrology will have to be placed at the top of the astrological tree (as it used to be in the past) and the more the State controls the individual, the truer this will be.'. The influences affecting the development of a town or city might be at odds with those affecting an individual living there, and consequently some people will prosper more in one town rather than another.

Glenys and I decided it would be an interesting exercise to look at the most important places in Somerset and see what their charts reveal. We chose Bath, Wells, Chard, Yeovil, Glastonbury, Bridgwater and Taunton. Their 'birthdates' varied a great deal – Wells 7th September 1201, Yeovil 3rd July 1854, Chard 29th July 1683 and so on – but armed with all the relevant information, a pile of reference books and various charts and tables, Glenys set to work. It proved to be more than interesting, it was fascinating.

'The first thing I did,' Glenys told me when she had finished her studies, 'was to create a composite list of Zodiac signs occupied by all of the ten planets of all of the towns put together. Immediately it showed a heavy concentration in certain Signs, whilst others were left almost empty. And the implications seemed very applicable to the whole county of Somerset as 'represented' by the activities of its combined towns.'

Glenys writes: *The first prominent Zodiac Sign to emerge was Cancer the Crab. At this point it is necessary to provide a comprehensive list of all occupations and matters 'ruled' by this Sign: Anything to do with the sea i.e. the Navy, fishing, boating hobbies and allied trades. Lakes and marshes. Food, shelter and clothing necessities. Catering – all branches. Shop keepers, especially groceries and bakeries. Milkmen or producers. Farmers' markets. Caring occupations i.e. retirement homes, nannies, nursing etc. Caring for homes i.e. carpenters, painters and decorators. Caring for home objects i.e. antiques. A great sense of history and the past i.e. caring for historical houses, museums, family trees, old traditions or ways of doing things. All preservation and conservation interests. Dark, hidden places as a protective shell or retreat. Places or things that are enclosed. Sense of humour and comedians.*

Historic Wells …

And the Garrick Head outside the eponymous hotel in Bath ...

This very homely, domesticated list (apart from the sea and Navy) seems to fit
Somerset very well. As a county it is rich in wonderful historic houses such as
Montacute, Lytes Cary, Barrington Court, Claverton Manor, Clevedon Court and
a variety of other 'cared for' dwellings at Georgian Bath etc. On the other hand it is
rather poor in castles, but then the warlike Zodiac Sign of Aries and possibly Scorpio
came very low on the composite list prepared. The older hill forts such as Cadbury
seem to fit better those 'places or things that are enclosed' for protection. Even Wells
classes as a protected enclosure as it is a city within a city and surrounded by high
walls.

The 'milkmen or producers' are well represented right through the food chain to the
famous Cheddar cheese.

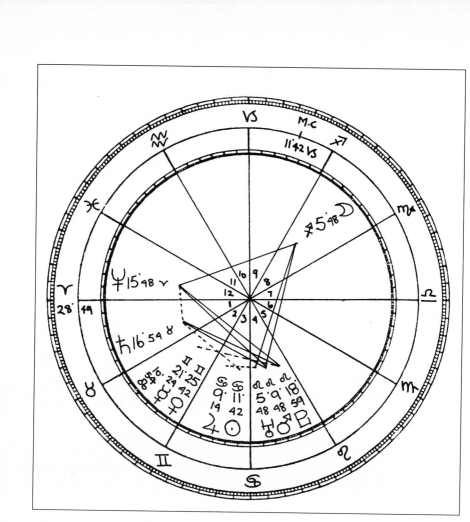

Glastonbury's Zodiac chart, in which intuition and psychic qualities can be found

The 'lakes and marshes' ascribed to Cancer are self-explanatory in connection with the drainage required in the low-lying wet areas of Somerset, resulting in later peat cutting and the withy-beds for basket making as domestic products.

Clothing has been an important industry from the old woollen days e.g. 'Cary', the tough woollen cloth produced at Castle Cary, through to the glove trade around Yeovil, footwear, sheepskin goods etc. But none of these industries is on a massive scale – the huge corporations ruled by Capricorn are absent and this was another Zodiac Sign fairly low on the composite list. Almost completely absent from the list was the Sign of Aquarius which rules modern technology and inventions, so it is not surprising that the existing woollen industry seemed lacking in the urge to capitalize

90

on the new mechanization of the Industrial Revolution which flourished instead in the North of England, leaving unrest and unemployment in Somerset. So 'clinging to the old traditions' in Cancerian fashion created a problem in this instance.

The 'protective shells and hidden retreats' fits perfectly with all the well known caves such as Cheddar and Wookey – the domestic homes of the day in Stone Age times.

Meanwhile, the Cancerian sense of humour must surely be at work when we consider that catering and bakeries come under its rulership, and that Somerset is the only county famous for having a king brought down to homely levels and burning the cakes whilst cooking!

The sea and the Navy are represented in Somerset, but more by way of catering to their needs i.e. sailmaking since Nelson's day at Crewkerne (a literal combination of two Cancerian occupations – 'clothes' for 'boats'), and also printing Admiralty charts at Taunton etc. Meanwhile, Admiral Blake was born at Bridgwater, but in the previously mentioned absence of heavier warlike zodiac signs from the composite list there have been no huge dockyards or famous people like Francis Drake or Walter Raleigh.

The Zodiac Sign of Gemini is a fairly strong runner-up to Cancer in the list. This Sign rules printers, writers and the travel industry (and vehicles) amongst other things. Its influence is obvious as a secondary theme to Cancer in Somerset, with all the printing industries and the making of paper at Watchet and Wookey. As expected from the presence of this Sign, writing does emerge in the person of Coleridge who lived at Stowey from 1797 to 1800 where he wrote 'The Ancient Mariner' (the sea again), and at Culbone he wrote 'Kubla Khan'. Not far from Coleridge's home, William and Dorothy Wordsworth lived at Alfoxton. Thackeray did some of his writing at Clevedon Court. Meanwhile, the 'travel and vehicles' side of this Air Sign has shown up as aircraft i.e. Westland aircraft works at Yeovil, not to mention John Stringfellow from Chard whose first power-driven aeroplane of 1848 is now in the London Science Museum.

Finally in this list of all the towns' planets put together, the Zodiac Sign of Pisces was about equal in strength to Gemini as a runner-up to the main Sign of Cancer. Some of the things ruled by Pisces are mysticism, religious sacrifice of the self often translated into helping the poor or sick or mentally ill, or into romance, music and art that can 'sway the masses'. (Pisces has two fish as a symbol and early Christians adopted it from the then already two thousand year old tradition of astrological philosophy to represent their religious ideals). The negative side of Pisces is a tendency to escapism via booze, drugs or tobacco etc, as opposed to other means to a 'higher' state of consciousness. Once again the application of the ancient meanings and principles contained in astrology have matched up to this study.

Apart from the obvious monastic traditions of Somerset and the romance attached to the Arthurian legends, it transpires that Dr John Westover lived in Porch House at Wedmore in the seventeenth century. He opened England's first private lunatic *asylum there and kindly offered little treats of tobacco to inmates. He gave medical help to the wounded of the Duke of Monmouth's fugitive army after the Battle of Sedgemoor, although pages from his detailed diary about this were ripped out. A wise decision as the 'hanging' Judge Jeffreys arrived soon after and used the village's stone cross as a gibbet (very Piscean – sacrifice of the followers of a cause).*

Even more fascinating is a tight triangle that can be drawn on the map between Wells, Glastonbury and Pilton (even a triangle has astrological significance – known as a Grand Trine aspect and reputed to denote 'ease' or a means of easing other problems). Over the centuries assorted pilgrims in garments ranging from medieval cloaks through to twinsets and pearls or 'hippie gear', and usually in groups, have been drawn to this little area to find a Piscean-type escape-route to their idea of an idealistic world. Regardless of whether they congregate at Wells for established tradition to the sound of a choir, or seek ancient 'vibes' or gurus in Glastonbury to the sound of a sitar, or are more recently joined together in potential communal deafness 'on a high' at Pilton, they are all seeking something from this little bit of Somerset.

Finally, it is worth mentioning that there were a surprising number of common links between the individual charts of Bath and Wells. Pisces, described above, is placed at the Midheaven of both cities. A perfect choice, as this point represents what a city (or person) aims at or becomes known for, and of course, they are linked by a shared bishop. Also, only these two cities had their Sun and Mercury placed in the Zodiac Sign of Virgo (neat and tidy and 'ruling' people of service to others, also well-kept written records and libraries). They are the only two cities to have the Water Sign of Cancer on the ascendant (denoting the things first noticed about a place, or person), and they are both famous for water i.e. the Roman baths and the water with swans surrounding the Bishop's Palace in Wells (derived from the Old English 'wellas' meaning 'springs'). Both cities have a difficult aspect between the Sun and Saturn. In personal charts this implies a lot of hard work with little wealth at the end of it, and also few or no children – not a bad description of the clergy, particularly years ago when they took vows of celibacy.

Meanwhile, Glastonbury 'stands out from the crowd' having a chart more heavily occupied by Fire and Air Signs and not much in common with Bath and Wells. It is a chart of pure intuition and very psychic and prophetic qualities. The conjunction of Sun and Jupiter implies religious kindness and upliftment to others. The planet Mars is in the Sign of Leo (strong, undeviating beliefs) but is placed in the fourth sector and badly aspected by Saturn (trouble over property, and the person's house likely to danger by fire, theft or sudden disruption – also trouble with property taxes). It is as though the wrath of Henry VIII was already 'written into the script'!

So much revealed by the 'birth' charts of these Somerset places! In fact Glenys herself is often amazed at what she discovers, how time and time again the influences of the planets shape and guide a life or a history.

It could be argued that astrology takes the mystery out of life, but others believe that in doing so it leaves an even greater one. For although men

92

have tried for hundreds, even thousands of years, to explain the complexities of the zodiac, no-one has succeeded. It is a universal mystery, and our Somerset mysteries are just a tiny part of it.

Taunton's commemoration of the Monmouth rebellion.

The Tudor Tavern, Taunton, where Judge Jeffreys is reputed to have lodged while hold-ing the courts at which he dealt with the rebels.

ABOUT EXMOOR
by Polly Lloyd
"'It is a cameo to be treasured," says Polly Lloyd who takes us on a reflective tour of this timeless corner of England.'
Book Journal

LEGENDS OF DORSET
by Polly Lloyd
The author explores legendary Dorset, visiting places as diverse as the Sacred Circle at Knowlton and Chesil Beach. Dorset is a mine of myth and folklore.
'Weird happenings . . .' Polly Lloyd delves through tales ranging from moving rocks to murders.
Ed Perkins, Southern Evening Echo

CURIOSITIES OF EXMOOR
by Felicity Young
'. . . a tour in words and pictures of the National Park embracing Somerset and Devon.'
Nancy Hammonds, Evening Herald
'Felicity Young, an artist who has contributed many drawings to Bossiney Books, makes her debut as an author with a beautiful description of Exmoor and its many delights.'
June Glover, South Hams Group of Newspapers

LEGENDS OF SOMERSET
by Sally Jones
65 photographs and drawings
Sally Jones travels across rich legendary landscapes. Words, drawings and photographs all combine to evoke a spirit of adventure.
'On the misty lands of the Somerset plain – as Sally Jones makes clear – history, legend and fantasy are inextricably mixed.'
Dan Lees, The Western Daily Press

SUPERNATURAL IN SOMERSET
by Rosemary Clinch
Atmospheres, healing, dowsing, fork-bending and strange encounters are only some of the subjects featured inside these pages. A book, destined to entertain and enlighten – one which will trigger discussion – certain to be applauded and attacked.
'...an illustrated study of strange encounters and extraordinary powers ...'
Somerset County Gazette

MYSTERIOUS PLACES
by Peter Underwood
Visits locations that 'seem to have been touched by a magic hand'. The man who has been called Britain's No. 1 ghost hunter reflects: *'We live in a very mysterious world . . .'*
'. . . an insight into some of the more mysterious places in the south west.'
David Elvidge, Launceston & Bude Gazette

WESTCOUNTRY HAUNTINGS
by Peter Underwood
'The Westcountry offers . . . just about every kind of ghostly manifestation . . .' *writes Peter Underwood, President of the Ghost Club. '. . . a chilling look at hauntings from Bristol to Cornwall . . . many of the accounts appear for the first time.'*
David Henderson, The Cornish Guardian

UNKNOWN SOMERSET
by Rosemary Clinch and Michael Williams
A journey across Somerset, visiting off-the-beaten-track places of interest. Many specially commissioned photographs by Julia Davey add to the spirit of adventure.
'Magical Somerset . . . from ley lines to fork-bending; a journey into the unknown . . . a guide which makes an Ordnance Survey map "a investment in adventure".'
Western Daily Press

THE QUANTOCKS
by Jillian Powell with photographs by Julia Davey
'Seen from Taunton or The Mendips, the Quantocks look timeless . . .' Sensitive combination of words and pictures produce a delightful portrait of the area.
'. . . a charming portrait of an area of great natural beauty and much historic interest.'
Somerset and Avon Life

We shall be pleased to send you our catalogue giving full details of our growing list of titles for Devon, Cornwall, Dorset, Somerset and Wiltshire and forthcoming publications. If you have difficulty in obtaining our titles, write direct to Bossiney Books, Land's End, St. Teath, Bodmin, Cornwall.